QUESTAR PUBLISHERS, INC.

THE BIBLE IN BUSINESS
©1989 by Ron Jenson
Published by Questar Publishers, Inc.

Printed in the United States of America

ISBN 0-945564-11-2

Cover Design by Jerry Werner

THE BIBLE IN BUSINESS

Compiled by Ron Jenson

QUESTAR PUBLISHERS, INC.
Sisters, Oregon

The Publishers of
THE BIBLE IN BUSINESS
welcome submitted chapters from readers
for any future additional volume of these devotional
thoughts for business men and women.

If you are a business person and wish to submit a chapter
written in the same format as that of the chapters in this
book, please send your manuscript, along with the name,
address, and phone number of your firm, to:

QUESTAR PUBLISHERS, INC.
Post Office Box 1720
Sisters, Oregon 97759

CONTRIBUTORS

FOREWORD

PERHAPS YOU HAVE NEVER thought of in quite this way, but it could be said of Jesus that He was a great model for managers. And His life story, the Bible, can be considered the most profound book about business ever written.

That is why I'm excited to recommend to you THE BIBLE IN BUSINESS. It's filled with principles and instruction from the Bible that can show you how to live HIS way in today's demanding world of commerce.

My friend Ron Jenson has gathered the reflections of business men and women who are daily confronted with the challenge of integrating their faith with their business life — a challenge that you, too, may be called to, just as I am.

As you read about God's direct involvement with business people, these daily selections will fire you with enthusiasm for the exciting journey of living out your Christianity among your peers. I especially like the "Thought for Today" — it's an effective way to quickly focus my thinking while I'm at work.

THE BIBLE IN BUSINESS is a book I won't just read... but read and live by.

KENNETH BLANCHARD

THE BIBLE
IN BUSINESS

THE COMMON TOUCH

"Who touched my clothes?"
"You see the people crowding against you,"
his disciples answered, "and yet you can ask,
'Who touched me?' " But Jesus kept looking
around to see who had done it.
Mark 5:30-32

INSIGHT

Jesus' encounter with the woman who touched His garments is familiar. We are quick to refer to it any time we discuss our Lord's uncanny sensitivity to the world around Him. We often attribute this ability to discern a common touch to His divine nature. But what does it reveal about His richly human ability to focus on the cares of others?

Pressed on all sides by the crowds, hurrying along to save the life of Jairus's daughter, Jesus revealed a rare insight into leadership. Not only did He sense the woman's touch, but He turned to her and gave her His full attention.

Over the years I have known and worked with several outstanding leaders in business and the professions. Those who command the greatest respect from their peers and the affection of their associates have one thing in common: When you are with them you know you are important to them. You sense that the things you discuss receive their full attention. They are not dis-

11

tracted by the numerous other items crowded into their
busy schedules.

ILLUSTRATION

Jack and JoAnn Hinckley, the parents of the young man
who attempted to assassinate President Reagan in
1981, had scarcely recovered from the consequences
of their son's tragic step into history when I agreed to
help them launch the American Mental Health Fund.
Letters poured in by the thousands, mostly from other
families whose loved ones were trapped in the puzzling
maze of mental illness. Jack and JoAnn were determined to turn their tragedy into triumph and help build
public awareness of this greatly misunderstood afflic-
tion.

After months of merciless pounding by the press, these
two courageous people reluctantly decided to go
public. We carefully scheduled the media appearances
and interviews for simultaneous airing and release. It
meant several days of difficult, emotionally wrenching
interviews in Washington D.C. and New York.

In the midst of the chaos, Jack suggested that we take
a relaxing walk through Central Park. As we strolled, we
talked about the interviews, the countless questions,
and the discomforting aspects of exposure. Suddenly
we found ourselves face to face with a vagrant. The
stench of urine and cheap wine made me wince as I
veered off the walkway to let him pass. Jack firmly
grasped my arm and led us straight ahead.

As we approached the ragged beggar, Jack removed his
hat and said brightly, "Hello!" The stunned pedestrian

looked up, smiled a toothless grin and returned the greeting.

"Did you see how young he was?" Jack asked. The man appeared to be in his early twenties. In his face was a lifetime of hurt, pain and rejection.

It had not been long since another young man — their son John — had wandered the streets of Nashville, New Haven and Washington D.C. I wondered if anyone had taken the time to speak to him. And if they had, would it have made a difference?

Although he didn't say so, Jack must have asked himself the same question — many times; but for one moment that day, he had made a difference in a life. Jack had discovered the power of the common touch.

Such encounters did not end in Central Park. Through-out the media tour I saw this "common touch principle" at work time and again. I watched one interviewer's cool veneer melt away as the Hinckleys listened to his story of a brother's struggle with schizophrenia. One well-known television newsman wept as he revealed that his chronically depressed daughter had taken her life with the gun he kept in a nightstand drawer. Another told of a troubled daughter and infant grand-daughter living as street people. No one forced them to tell their stories. They simply yielded to the common touch.

The Hinckleys are not the only possessors of this powerful human quality. My list includes champions of business and industry, educators, attorneys, and legisla-tors — men and women who set aside their own agendas long enough to touch another life.

CHALLENGE

Is your leadership style marked by a sincere consideration of others? Are you able to look beyond your personal or organizational goals and see other, often deeper, things at work? Certainly it takes remarkable discipline and sacrifice. But it also yields rich rewards in individual lives.

THOUGHT FOR TODAY

Jesus did not let a hectic schedule crowd out valuable encounters with others. Wherever He was, He was one-hundred-percent present, giving dignity to individuals through the common touch.

by Jim Roberts
Eckerd Family Foundation
Clearwater, Florida

GOD'S GAUNTLET

"Bring the whole tithe into the storehouse...
Test me in this," says the LORD Almighty, "and see
if I will not throw open the floodgates of heaven
and pour out so much blessing that you
will not have room enough for it."
Malachi 3:10

INSIGHT

Many leaders are reluctant to talk about giving money.
But I view fund-raising as an opportunity to teach
people to pick up the gauntlet dropped by God; I
believe God is saying, "Test Me, prove Me, outgive Me."
Often this means that we are asking people to make
commitments with nothing humanly tangible to back up
those commitments. But we start from the standpoint
that God owns everything we have, and He's not going
to allow us to give it all away without replenishing it.

ILLUSTRATION

I have observed that one of the most important rules in
raising funds is **making sure you ask for enough.** Let
me be more blunt. I think that every "ask" should be
large enough to make the prospect blanch. A good rule
of thumb: If you don't drain the color out of the face,
you haven't gone high enough. I have seen a lot of

people blanch! However, thankfully, I have never inspired one cardiac arrest.

It's my personal experience that people respond to a challenge; people respond to something special if you can convince them that there is indeed a very special need. If you have a credible program, and if they have the ability to be associated with it at the level that you've asked, they will do it — and they will indeed experience great joy when they do.

Over dinner one evening I asked a man for one million dollars. When he heard the figure, he just looked at me, and beads of perspiration appeared on his upper lip. Finally he said, "That's a lot of money." And that's all he said to me for the next eight months. A year passed, and he gave us $1 million. The moment he gave it, everything he touched came up roses.

I'm not saying this will always be the case — I'm not preaching a gospel of prosperity — but in his case, there were tangible outcomes, the windows of heaven opened, and he experienced a land of milk and honey! His bank accounts grew, his investments tripled, everything he touched turned to gold.

He is a very spiritual man, and at this point in his life he said, "God has blessed my gift." About eight months later he came back to me without any prompting on my part, and pledged a second million dollars.

This all happened while I served at Eastern College and Seminary. About three months before I left my position there, I was spending a day with him at his home and he brought up the subject on his own a second time. These are his exact words: "Bob, I have more money to give, can you help me?" I spent most of that day writing a proposal, one that we discussed that night, and before the evening was over, he had pledged an additional five million dollars.

CHALLENGE

It's not the **amount** of money that's important to God. God doesn't need our money. Don't ever be so arrogant or presumptuous to think that God needs your cash in order for Him to usher in His kingdom. God only wants you to give, so He can open those windows of heaven and bless you in return. God wants a person's heart much more than He'll ever want their money. A gift made from a pure heart, a proper attitude, a godly motivation will not return void, but will accomplish what God wants it to accomplish.

For the Christian, sacrificial giving is really the only kind of giving that works. The concept of sacrifice is woven throughout Scripture and finds its ultimate incarnation in the death of Jesus. The concept of giving and the concept of sacrifice are so intertwined that I have absolutely no reluctance to use the phrase "sacrificial giving."

If we, or those we influence, merely give "leftovers" from discretionary income, we and they are denied the joy God has promised to return. And if we ask people only to give what they can easily spare from their riches, they will never experience God's fullest blessings. God wants to work with children of faith. He wants some evidence in our life that we will follow Him, that we will support the work of the kingdom out of obedience and our love for Him. He wants us to give, not because He needs the money, but because in a very real way it is a mark of our spiritual maturity. And the spiritually mature person will experience joy.

THOUGHT FOR TODAY

All God asks is that we take Him at His word. "Test me...and see if I will not throw open the floodgates of heaven and pour out so much blessing that you will not have room enough for it."

by Robert Seiple
World Vision
Monrovia, California

'GLAD YOU ASKED!'

Whatever happens, conduct yourselves in a
manner worthy of the gospel of Christ.
Philippians 1:27

INSIGHT

Christ calls us to the High Road of human conduct and
behavior. He calls us to be a visibly different people
who stand tall — living what we believe.

ILLUSTRATION

After the infamous Watergate scandal, the Secretary of
the Air Force espoused a new ethical standard to be
applied throughout the government. Today, with our
litany of daily scandals — from Pentagon overspending,
to Wall Street insider trading, to the defective pair of car
tires I bought last week — I could not help remember-
ing the Secretary's challenging standard, and wishing it
were used by everyone, everywhere.

It is, in reality, a secularized version of Paul's admonition to the Philippians. It is called the "Glad you asked!"
standard. And it says:

Let each of your actions be of such high quality,
purity, and good faith that if the crew from
CBS's "60 Minutes" program — or Sam Donald-

son, or Ralph Nader, or your company's auditor,
or your son or daughter — should ask you
about it, you can truthfully and cheerfully say,
"I'm glad you asked! We're proud of what we
are doing, and I'd like nothing better than to
share the whole file in this matter with you, and
to give you the complete background on our
reasoning."

Rotary International, of which I have been a part for
many years, achieves the same end with its "Four Way
Test":

"Of the things we think, say, or do...ASK:

1. Is it the TRUTH?
2. Is it FAIR to all concerned?
3. Will it build GOOD WILL and BETTER
   FRIENDSHIPS?
4. Will it be BENEFICIAL to all concerned?"

CHALLENGE

Our challenge in everything we do, large or small, is to
strive to bring honor and glory to His name, by being
obedient to the gospel of Christ Jesus; and to do this in
such a way that we encourage others, Christians and
non-Christians alike, to follow the High Road of the Four
Way Test and the "Glad you asked!" standard.

From our witness, may we provoke others to ask who
our Lord is.

Thought for Today

Let all of my actions in business or personal affairs be such that, if asked by "60 Minutes" or by Jesus Christ, I can truthfully and cheerfully say, "I'm glad you asked!"

by C. Neal Johnson
First National Bank
Artesia, New Mexico

HEART-TALK
WITH THE FATHER

In the same way, the Spirit helps us in our
weakness. We do not know what we ought to pray,
but the Spirit himself intercedes for us with groans
that words cannot express. And he who searches
our hearts knows the mind of the Spirit, because
the Spirit intercedes for the saints
in accordance with God's will.
Romans 8:26-27

INSIGHT

Secrets. We all have them. Secret thoughts, feelings,
fears and memories we simply can't tell anyone. Yet, we
feel that if we don't share them we'll explode...burst!

These are the things we can tell our Father in heaven.
Sometimes it helps to write out these things because
writing is often easier than verbalizing, and can be a
key to understanding our own inner feelings more
clearly.

But no matter how well we are able to express ourselves, we are fortunate in that the Holy Spirit of God
understands even our groanings, and can interpret
them to the Father. We don't have to be articulate; we
don't even have to put it into words. He knows our
hearts.

ILLUSTRATION

When Jesus was on earth, He modeled this kind of openness with the Father. While He was in the desert He said, "Now my heart is troubled, and what shall I say, Father, save Me from this hour? No, it is for this reason I came to this hour. Father glorify Your Name!" (John 12:27) And in the Garden of Gethsemane, as He anticipated His own crucifixion, the Scripture tells us He sweat drops of blood. He expressed his deepest feelings to His Father as He prayed, "Father, if it be possible, let this cup pass from Me. But not My will, but Thine be done." Then on the cross His heart cried out, "My God, My God, why have You forsaken Me?" Jesus had the ability to tell what was in His deepest being to the Father...sometimes in a groan or a cry, sometimes in a question, sometimes in a statement.

Heart-talk with the Father frequently gives us new perspective and options. It's like the experience we have each had of talking with a friend who remains silent, but we're able to say, "It helped just to talk about it." Often, the Father talks to us. Dr. Bill Bright, Founder and President of Campus Crusade describes the Father's communication as "illumination, where things just begin to make sense to us; and instructions, where God actually gives us certain perspectives."

CHALLENGE

In your next heart-talk with the Father try talking about:
- The most profound disappointment you've ever experienced.

- Hopes and dreams others would not understand.
- Broken relationships that have left you emotionally devastated.
- Decisions or problems you are struggling with.
- Feelings others could not help you work through right now.
- Confessions of inadequacy, self-doubt, temptation, failure.
- Lingering questions you've always wanted to ask.

THOUGHT FOR TODAY

Heart-talk with the Father promises to help us gain an eternal perspective on our situation. By simply turning to God we are moving from the limitations of time to a perspective enlarged by eternity.

by Bobb Biehl
Masterplanning Group International
Laguna Niguel, California

HIGHER GROUND

But I tell you who hear me: Love your enemies,
do good to those who hate you, bless those who
curse you, pray for those who mistreat you.
Luke 6:27

INSIGHT

Jesus is clearly challenging us to be active in "negative"
relationships — It is essential that we be so attuned to
His Spirit as to be positively involved in these relationships, rather than neutral or evasive.

ILLUSTRATION

A few years ago I worked for a decentralized company
where certain individuals built up power bases. One
person, who had access to my business and personal
files, began gossiping about me and spreading lies and
innuendos. Soon, this person had recruited a handful
of people who intensified this activity.

My reaction to this situation was very intense. I found
myself not only preoccupied with trying to figure out
how to "set the record straight," but feeling hate toward
these people. Also, since I was an officer of the
company, I kept thinking, *I have the power to fire
these people.* As I thought this, the words of the Lord
pierced my mind: "You have no power apart from

CHRIST UNITED METHODIST CHURCH
4488 POPLAR AVENUE
MEMPHIS, TENNESSEE 38117

Me...pray for those who mistreat you...love your enemies." I certainly preferred to study these words in my devotions rather than apply them in this difficult environment.

Against my will, I finally began to pray for the situation and the people involved. In addition, I started to work with the "leader" of this group rather than isolate myself from her. I included her in planning meetings, asked her advice on various matters and generally tried to be positively proactive in the situation. One day this same woman came up to me and showed me a picture of herself years earlier when she was 150 pounds heavier, and said, "This is me." The barriers of hate and mistrust had been broken down. She was reaching out for understanding and love. Her self-esteem had been so low that she would hate someone who was a threat to her power base.

As it turned out, within a few months almost all of the individuals involved were transferred, quit, or were fired (by someone other than myself). I am often reminded of the Lord's words:"Apart from Me, you can do nothing." This painful incident reminds me that the flesh is bent towards selfishness and destruction rather than love and reconciliation. I wanted so badly to fire these individuals and strongly believed it would have been right. The Lord protected me by prompting me to pray and giving me the power to love when I wanted to hate.

CHALLENGE

Clearly, we are commanded to love and pray for our enemies. Who are your enemies? Consider writing down their names and mentioning each of them in your prayers. Ask God for wisdom and understanding regarding who these people are and why they act like they do. Now the tough part — think of specific ways that you can reach out and humble yourself before them. Remember, we have no power apart from Him.

THOUGHT FOR TODAY

When we were His enemies, God through Jesus Christ reached out and humbly sacrificed Himself. My enemy today can be my brother or sister in the Lord tomorrow.

by John Alexander
Noro International
Atlanta

THE KEY

One of them...tested him with this
question: "Teacher, which is the greatest
commandment in the Law?"
Jesus replied: " 'Love the Lord your God
with all your heart and with all your soul
and with all your mind.' This is the first
and greatest commandment. And the second
is like it: 'Love your neighbor as yourself.' "
Matthew 22:35-38

INSIGHT

God does not confuse us as to what it takes to follow
Him. Here Jesus tells us the essence of belonging to
Him. These are the essentials. Other things are sec-
ondary.

ILLUSTRATION

Over the years I have been active in at least six Christ-
centered churches. My consulting work has allowed me
to get close to over a dozen national parachurch organizations. In different ways, the implied or spoken rules
usually signal that a particular set of beliefs, attitudes or
behaviors is required for "full membership." In various
ways, groups develop long lists of do's and don'ts. The
workplace then adds all of its expectations. We can

indeed become overwhelmed by what God seems to be requiring.

Jesus is more clear. Just love God, He says. Sounds simple. But in our world this can be the most difficult commitment. Why not just tithe? Attend prayer meetings? Serve on the board of elders?

Mother Teresa wrote a letter to an American. She asked for prayer that her deep involvement in helping the poor not keep her from loving God. How about us? How important to us is loving God?

How do we muster up the love God asks us to have? He Himself provides the answer. He sent His only Son to assume the defeat we deserve. Then He sent His Holy Spirit to help us live the way He wants us to.

Loving God? The Bible says the secret of this mystery is *Christ in us.*

Frankly, it is difficult for me to understand that I cannot meet God's test alone. By faith I need to yield to His love and simply give Him mine. How unlike the way the world encourages us to think!

CHALLENGE

Are you tired of trying to do everything that well-meaning believers suggest you should do? *Love God.*

Are you treading water trying to discover what life is all about? *Love God.*

Do you want to experience the joy of belonging to Him in your work, family, leisure, and church? *Love God* with all your heart, soul, and mind.

THOUGHT FOR TODAY

Loving God is the key to our deepest longings.

by Robert Andringa
CEO Services Group
Englewood, Colorado

CAPTIVE TO HIS LOVE

See to it that no one takes you captive through
hollow and deceptive philosophy, which depends
on human tradition and the basic principles of this
world rather than on Christ.
Colossians 2:8

INSIGHT

In every undertaking we will encounter a negative force
and a positive force at work. The negative force, hollow
and deceptive while depending on human tradition and
worldly principles, is based upon the motive of greed.
It's a "What's in it for me?" philosophy. And it inevitably
leads to disappointment and disillusion.

The positive force is dependent on living out biblical
principles with God's Spirit as the energizer. It is based
on love and leads to a desire to serve and help others
achieve their goals. The inevitable results will be satisfaction abounding in peace and joy.

ILLUSTRATION

My business career has been evenly divided between
these two philosophies — and I have the battle scars to
prove it. In the first eleven years of my career I earned
and lost a fortune because I was motivated by greed.
My goals were to build a net worth in excess of one

million dollars by the age of thirty-five — and to be recognized for it.

The results were predictable. Upon graduation from college, I worked very long hours. My marriage ended in divorce. I encountered repeated frustration in the pursuit of my goals, but at the age of thirty-five I had achieved them. I had remarried and was living on a five-acre estate with a tennis court and indoor pool. My wife and I both drove luxury cars.

One year later we moved west with thousands of dollars of debts and a mere five hundred dollars in our pockets. I started over again, and during the next few years built a restaurant company of six fast-food and five seafood operations. Once again I was working crazy hours seven days a week, with no time for a young family that I loved very much. I became associated with a couple of dishonest and bickering partners. I was unhappy and without peace in my life.

With the help of a few caring friends — who were sent into my life by the Lord even before I knew Him personally — I was enabled to realize that I was being deceived by a wrong philosophy, just like the frog in the well-known analogy: If you boil a pan of water and put a frog in it, the frog will jump out. But if you put the frog in the water and then heat it slowly, the frog will adjust its body temperature to match the water as it heats up. The frog will continue to adjust until he is dead.

A Christian businessman explained to me God's plan for my life through Jesus Christ. He also helped me begin to understand that the Bible contains an abundance of principles for us to apply here on earth. During the next eleven years of my life I witnessed the results of the application of these principles based on love. Because God first loved me and has rescued me from a life of futility, I now love Him and desire to please Him.

I have seen my wife and each of our three children become Christians. My in-laws' marriage has been restored. My parents became Christians in their mid-sixties. My father has been healed of cancer, and there have been many other answers to prayer in my personal life.

Professionally, I have observed God enabling us to increase our annual sales 450 percent during the last eight years. As we have consistently applied God's principles in the areas of employee compensation and recognition, providing for their needs, and providing them an enjoyable work environment, we have seen more than twenty of them become Christians. As we have applied those same principles in working with our suppliers, such as advising them on billing errors where they shorted themselves, we have encountered exceptional favor, and one of these suppliers committed his life to the Lord during a breakfast meeting.

CHALLENGE

Do you desire a business founded upon principles of the world or a business founded upon the rock-steady principles of God?

Jesus says: "Therefore everyone who hears these words of Mine and puts them into practice is like a wise man who built his house on the rock. The rain came down, the streams rose, and the winds blew and beat against that house; yet it did not fall, because it had its foundation on the rock" (Matthew 7:24-25).

THOUGHT FOR TODAY

In each of the decisions I will face today, I will ask myself "How can I best serve others?" and "How can I express my love for Jesus Christ through my actions and responses to this situation?"

by Armand Dauplaise
Snack Hostess, Inc.
Fairfax, Virginia

PROVEN WORTH

For he chose us in him before the creation of the
world to be holy and blameless in his sight...in
order that we, who were the first to hope in Christ,
might be for the praise of his glory.
Ephesians 1:4,12

INSIGHT

You know what it is to feel the pressure of those around
you who demand that you meet certain criteria in order
to be deemed acceptable, to be considered successful.
You must prove your worth by "doing." The effectiveness of your "doing" determines the measure to which
you will be acceptable. God's plan and economy are
different. He places greater emphasis on "being" than
He does on "doing." He says He chose you as a unique
object of His infinite love. He says you are of tremendous worth, totally acceptable in His Son.

ILLUSTRATION

I grew up the youngest of two brothers. My earliest rec-
ollections of childhood are my parents helping my
brother with his homework at the kitchen table. He
found schoolwork difficult and my parents were simply
doing what was necessary to help him make his grades.
They were, of course, only doing what caring and concerned parents should for a child needing their atten-

tion. But little boys don't think as much as they feel. I realize now that I mistakenly interpreted the time and attention which my parents gave my brother as their greater love and interest for him than for me.

Early in my life I developed an independent, self-reliant and competitive spirit. I prided myself on the fact that I didn't need my parents' help with schoolwork. I was a "straight-A" student. This effort — to be an achiever, to be successful, to pay the price to be the best I could be — was, unknowingly for many years, an attempt to prove my worth to myself. Even after accepting Christ as Savior, I found myself driven to succeed, to gain the applause and approval of those around me. I continued to seek a sense of self-worth, a sense of being accepted because of my accomplishments.

A few years ago, at forty years of age, I was diagnosed as an asthmatic. With the best medical technology available to me, my condition deteriorated. Twice I found myself in a hospital emergency room, gasping for breath. I shall never forget the night God spoke to me in an inaudible but clear voice: "Jay, you've concentrated on the doing, and you've had success, but look at the toll your striving has taken on your flesh. Let Me do it." That was the beginning of a healing process — physically, emotionally, and spiritually — when medical technology was useless.

I no longer need the breathing machines. I am experiencing strength and vitality I've not known for years. But, more importantly, I am experiencing healing of my spirit. What a relief to know I don't have to prove my worth to others or to myself! I began to believe God's Word that He loves me and delights in me. When I understood God valued me enough to give His only Son to die for me, I began to accept myself just as I am.

CHALLENGE

No amount of "doing" can ever bring you a sense of complete fulfillment. God loves you! You don't have to prove anything to Him. The pressure is off. This truth has been eloquently spoken in the flesh through Jesus Christ.

THOUGHT FOR TODAY

Your Creator thinks you are priceless. Rest in His love and rejoice in His acceptance of who you are today.

by James Ahleman
Vienna, Virginia

SUCCESS IS FROM THE LORD

The God of heaven will give us success.
We his servants will start rebuilding.
Nehemiah 2:20

INSIGHT

Christian business men and women know that with God all things are possible. We're not fighting the world or "principalities" alone. Knowing this leads to a realization that our greatest successes are best described as God's grace.

ILLUSTRATION

It has taken me decades to figure out the message of the story of Nehemiah. Like others, I believed success was the reward for hard work and long hours. I figured I earned it myself. However, careful study of the facts has revealed that the three biggest financial successes of my life were not due to my efforts at all. In fact, while I was sweating the small deals, the three biggies fell into my lap.

Like Nehemiah, we should get into harmony with God's will. What's so special about Nehemiah?

- He had a sense of mission.
- He prayed about it.
- He waited for God's timing.
- He made firsthand investigations.
- He acted confidently in the Lord.
- He identified himself as God's servant.
- He set an attainable goal.
- He rearranged priorities in order to reach it.
- He did not become discouraged.

I now pray often for God's direction in my life. I pray for His guidance. I do this with the determination of a bulldog. Why? Because I want every moment remaining in my life on this earth to glorify God and reflect eternal values.

CHALLENGE

Read the entire book of Nehemiah...read it again and again and again. As you do so, put yourself into his sandals and learn to do things his way. Then put Nehemiah into your wingtips (or loafers) and ask God to show you how to best conduct your life. Role-play; then pray...then DO IT!

Our world is crying for leaders who will arise and build, doing God's will today.

THOUGHT FOR TODAY

Getting into harmony with God's will requires faith. The world tells us lies by the thousands — and too often we

believe them. Focus — in faith — on God's will. And
remember that success is His gift.

by Carl Schuele
KRUZ Stereo
Santa Barbara, California

A WORKOUT

I'm not just shadow-boxing or playing around.
Like an athlete I punish my body, treating it
roughly, training it to do what it should, not what it
wants to. Otherwise I fear that after enlisting others
for the race, I myself might be declared unfit and
ordered to stand aside.
1 Corinthians 9:26-27, THE LIVING BIBLE

INSIGHT

For some reason the world really doesn't expect to see
Christians work hard. Non-Christians tend to see Christians as sissies, wimps, or pushovers. But a Christian
should run his or her race to win, to gain first place in
business or athletics, to be the best employee possible,
the best truck driver, the best advertising agency
person, the best neighbor, the best church member, the
best homemaker. We should run with purpose, setting
goals, eyeing the mark, denying self, and being the best
Christian we can possibly be.

ILLUSTRATION

My wife and I know a number of professional athletes
here in Seattle and around the country. We see how
hard they work before the cheers begin. They punish
their bodies by making them do things they don't want

to do, like running, lifting weights, doing push-ups, working out on exercise equipment, and then running some more.

Part of our "exercise" as Christians includes programming our minds to act in the right way automatically. A football coach wants to have his players get to a point where they don't have to think when they go to make a block or set up a defense. He wants them to react instinctively. That's the way God wants us to act too. If we preprogram ourselves with the Word, then we can act the right way when faced with a temptation, trial, surprise, or someone cutting us off on the freeway. God wants us to act instinctively so we can react His way, rather than reacting in our natural way.

Having that kind of response takes practice — disciplined training. God gives us His grace and spiritual power to enable us to change, but we still must do our part.

We know God loves us and will not allow anything to come into our lives that is not in our best interest. He goes through the problem with us, because the Holy Spirit is right there inside us, filling our hearts with the knowledge of God's love. But we can't trust someone we don't know. How can we trust God with problems if we don't know Him? And how can we know Him without getting into the Bible on a regular basis? And how can we get into the Bible on a regular basis without working at it?

CHALLENGE

Time is too short to play games in the Christian life. We can't have one foot on the dock and one foot on the ship and expect to go anywhere. As I've heard Chuck Swindoll say, some of us have too much of the world to be comfortable with Christ, and too much of Christ to be comfortable in the world.

I used to work with a man who acted and sounded like a Christian when he was with Christians, but when he was with non-Christians he acted and sounded just like one of them. The non-Christians in his life knew he should not be involved in some of the things he was doing, yet I suppose it gave them some comfort to drag him down a bit. The Christians in his life knew he was a fake because his walk didn't match his talk. He was basically a lazy, worldly Christian.

We can't be like that if we mean business about transforming our thoughts and actions, knowing the Bible, and knowing and trusting God.

THOUGHT FOR TODAY

It takes effort — but amazingly enough, once we truly want to know and trust God, and are committed to working hard at learning what the Bible says about Him and putting His precepts into practice, He rewards us with rich insights and blessings far beyond what our attempts deserve.

He's that kind of God!

by Chuck Snyder
Chuck Snyder Advertising
Seattle
from his book I PRAYED FOR PATIENCE —
AND OTHER HORROR STORIES
(Questar, 1989)

YOU CAN'T OUTGIVE GOD

Give, and it will be given to you. A good measure, pressed down, shaken together and running over, will be poured into your lap. For with the measure you use, it will be measured to you.
Luke 6:38

INSIGHT

You can't outgive God. His resources are fully reliable, abundant, and freely offered on your behalf.

ILLUSTRATION

The church I was attending needed an educational building to support its rapid growth. But at the rate the fund was growing, those children would have been grandparents before the building was completed! The chairman of the building committee approached me one Sunday and asked if I would give a short talk urging contributions. He said, "Mary Kay, you do believe that children should be brought up in the church, don't you?"

"Yes, of course," I answered.

"Well then, say so!" he responded. I put it on my calendar and out of my mind.

Late one Saturday night I arrived home from a tiring business trip and overslept the next morning. I checked my calendar only to find that it was the day I had agreed to speak. There was no time to prepare. I asked God to give me the right words. The Lord has never spoken to me personally as He has to some people but suddenly, after that prayer, the strongest thought I've ever had in my life came to me. **"Tell the congregation you will match whatever they give today!"** The thought was so shocking to me, I backed up from the mirror where I was putting on my makeup and thought, *Oh Lord, I can't do that!* But the thought persisted.

The choir was already in place when I entered the sanctuary, and I was immediately called to the pulpit. As I went up the steps, I had no idea what I would say. I simply talked of my early years teaching beginners and how important I thought it was for children to be brought up in the church. Then I followed God's command and offered to match the congregation's gifts that day. Since our company is run on a cash basis, I asked for cash or checks — no pledges. There seemed to be no special response, and I felt as I left the pulpit that I had failed to get my message across.

The next morning, feeling depressed by my failure, I was sitting at my desk when the chairman of the building committee called. "We didn't expect what happened," he said, "and we know you didn't; so we had a meeting and voted that you should not be held to your offer." When I asked how much was given — I was thinking perhaps a thousand dollars, maybe even five thousand or ten thousand — he reiterated that they did not expect me to keep my promise.

Finally, asking if I were sitting down, he told me the amount was $111,097. There was a silence on my end of the line as I wondered where I could come up with

$111,097 that day. (Since I had asked for cash the same day from the congregation, I felt I also had to respond in that manner.) After a few moments the building chairman said, "Well?"

"I said I would, so I will," I replied, and we hung up. I bowed my head and asked God's help in finding a way to meet this obligation.

Less than five minutes passed. The next phone call was from my son, who manages my financial affairs. He was very excited. "Mother," he said, "you remember a few months back I told you I was going to invest in some oil wells for you? I told you that only about one in nine actually comes in, but that perhaps it could be a tax write-off? Well," he continued, "they both came in and they are gushers. I have the first royalty check for over $100,000!"

CHALLENGE

Dr. Robert Schuller has used an analogy which reminds me of this miracle in my life: "If we shovel our resources in with our little shovel, God will shovel them back with his big shovel."

THOUGHT FOR TODAY

I can never be too bold in my expectations of God's love and power.

by Mary Kay Ash
Mary Kay Cosmetics
Dallas

GOD IS IN CONTROL

"For I know the plans I have for you," declares the
LORD, "plans to prosper you and not to harm you,
plans to give you hope and a future."
Jeremiah 29:11

INSIGHT

God knows what lies in front of us. He can never be
taken by surprise. His plans for us are good, and only
for our best. Because of this, you and I have hope and
security, particularly during the dark times of our lives.

ILLUSTRATION

The year 1987 was a tough one for me. A real estate
investment project I had worked on for three years had
the loan coming due and the market was lousy. It
needed to be sold and I went everywhere trying to sell
it. Even a trip to Europe found people uninterested in
excellently located, low-priced real estate.

Coming back from that trip, I found the oldest of my
four children extremely sick. As I finally entered stress-
ful negotiations in the sale of my real estate, my mother
also became ill. Two weeks later I was hit by a careless
driver who sent me to the hospital and destroyed my
car. In excruciating pain, I continued negotiations.

The property transaction went through, and that same month we sold our home, purchased a new one, moved my office, and welcomed a fifth child into our family. But the result of this stress was rock-bottom depression for me. I had no desire to communicate with my family or anyone else. I experienced chest pains, sleeplessness, tingling in my limbs, nausea, and a racing heartbeat. For the first time in my life I identified with the depths of emotion that cause a person to consider suicide. Because of my knowledge of God, that was not an option for me, yet I understood the feelings.

I left town for a week with nothing but my Bible. I read it throughout the day and took long walks. In the darkness of a sleepless night I meditated on Jeremiah 29:11. Did God have a plan for me? If so, could I trust the eternal God for even one more hour? Could he possibly give me peace in the chaos of my soul?

That week God confirmed that he was in control and had a good plan for me. I met three people who turned my life in His direction. The first was a businessman who had experienced the same kinds of stresses and the same depression I was going through. His advice to me was, "You must let go of the ownership of everything in your life. Release it all to God. He owns it all anyway and has ultimate control over it."

This sounded too simple. Yet I sat down and listed everything that "belonged" to me: my wife, my children, material possessions, my abilities, my health. Once and for all, I consciously gave all these to God and acknowledged His power to do whatever He willed. The only thing remaining was my own spirit, and I now realized He had bought that at a precious price, the death of His Son, Jesus, on the cross. This sacrifice guaranteed to me life with Him for all eternity.

The second person who helped me that week was a Bible teacher who confirmed that power to rise above circumstances comes through spending time with the power source — God Himself. That week alone gave me a good start on renewing this truth in my life.

The third person who helped turn my life around was a young recent graduate of the local university. I was reminded by him that God wants us to live one day at a time and enjoy that one day. "Plan fun into some part of the day," he encouraged me. "Certainly, you can do this if you realize God is in control. The seriousness of any situation finally falls on his shoulders, not yours." He told me most of His classmates were on their way to million-dollar careers, yet most of them were forgetting to enjoy each new day as a gift of God.

CHALLENGE

Are you caught up in an unpleasant situation right now? Believe that God has a good plan for you! In Jeremiah 29, verses 12 and 13 go on to say that if you call on God, He will listen; when you seek Him with all your heart, you will find Him.

THOUGHT FOR TODAY

God cares for you and me much more than we imagine. He has proven it by dying for us and He will prove it in the future by unfolding His good plan one day at a time.

by Henry Morgan
Henry Morgan & Co.
Dallas

DARE TO BE A DANIEL IN A VULNERABLE WORLD

Now Daniel so distinguished himself among the administrators and the satraps by his exceptional qualities that the king planned to set him over the whole kingdom. At this, the administrators and the satraps tried to find grounds for charges against Daniel...but they...could find no corruption in him, because he was trustworthy and neither corrupt nor negligent...

So (they) went as a group to the king and said: "(We) have all agreed that the king should issue an edict and enforce the decree that anyone who prays to any god or man during the next thirty days, except to you, O king, shall be thrown into the lions' den"...So King Darius put the decree in writing.

Now when Daniel learned that the decree had been published, he went home...Three times a day he got down on his knees and prayed, giving thanks to his God, just as he had done before. Then these men went as a group and found Daniel praying and asking God for help...So the king gave the order, and they brought Daniel and threw him into the lions' den...
Daniel 6:3-16

INSIGHT

There are many opportunities to hedge on honesty in business dealing, to walk on the edge between right and wrong. God has called us to be above reproach in an unbelieving world. His expectation applies to all aspects of our lives, including business. We are to be completely above reproach. Anything less is unacceptable. Daniel could easily have changed his worship habits for thirty days, but he would not compromise his faith. Neither should we.

ILLUSTRATION

Living in a part of the country that recently changed from economic boom to near-depression, I have watched Christian brothers becoming involved in less than ethical business dealings, in order to maintain the prosperity they enjoyed a few short years ago. Not that the dealings were blatantly wrong or sinful, they just weren't clearly right. As a result of their involvement, some found themselves entangled in situations that hurt them monetarily, or damaged their reputation, or disturbed their peace-of-mind.

I recently found myself in a position where I was tempted to compromise ethical standards. My advertising agency was asked to create an advertising campaign for a drug product which could be used as an aphrodisiac. It wasn't illegal or dishonest, but it was clear in my mind the drug could be advertised and used in ways which were not glorifying to God.

At the outset of the first meeting with my client, my spirit was troubled. Yet I suppressed my feelings, lured by the prospect of significant financial gain. (I should add that I was also uncomfortable about the quality of men with whom I was dealing.) After two weeks of rationalizing to myself why it was alright to handle this product, I concluded that the money was not worth the loss of peace I was experiencing. My company resigned the account and my peace-of-mind returned.

Would my Christian witness have been damaged by continued association with this product? Luckily, I will never have to find out. But the point is, I should never have allowed myself to be placed in that position of risk. I knew going in I should not be involved with that company, and my spirit kept prompting me to get out. But, because I could rationalize that the situation was not unethical or illegal, I allowed the lure of monetary gain to hold me there too long.

Daniel, faced with a similar yet far more severe situation, did not compromise his faith in any way. He could have rationalized away a change in his worship habits, in order to protect his life. He could have said to himself, "Surely God will understand if I don't pray to Him for just thirty days." After all, these were pretty extreme circumstances!

We are living in extreme circumstances today. The permissiveness of our society creates numerous opportunities to get into situations which will not glorify God. Behavior unspeakable a few short years ago is acceptable today. And the pressure to be successful is greater than ever.

Almost daily we read about men in powerful positions who fall prey to pride, greed or lust. Unfortunately, some of these men are Christians. I would suspect most of them did not plan to sin; but because they allowed themselves to get in positions where they were vulnerable, they lost out to the power of Satan. Had they followed his example and not compromised their standards, they could have avoided the heartache they are now experiencing.

CHALLENGE

As Christians in the business world, our mandate is clear: We must not enter business dealings which can lead us to compromise our faith. We must stay constantly aware that, given today's business climate, we can easily find ourselves in positions of vulnerability. It is not good enough to merely avoid dishonesty. We must make a clear stand for what is right in everything we do.

THOUGHT FOR TODAY

If we consider ourselves ambassadors for the living God, we will conduct our businesses in a manner that is completely and unequivocally above reproach.

by Paul Flowers
Flowers Marketing & Advertising, Inc.
Dallas

EVIDENCE OF PRIORITIES

A new commandment I give you: Love one
another. As I have loved you, so you
must love one another. All men will
know that you are my disciples
if you love one another.
John 13:34-35

INSIGHT

Christianity is not a religion, but a relationship. Just as
Jesus spent time developing intimate relationships with
the special people God called Him to disciple during
His time on earth, I believe God calls us to develop
intimate relationships with people.

The logistics of doing that in an era of breakfast, lunch
and dinner meetings, car telephones, video teleconfer-
ences and FAX machines are difficult indeed. Yet our
response to this challenge is absolutely crucial in deter-
mining the direction, satisfaction, and ultimate success
of our lives.

ILLUSTRATION

"Busyness" has become a status symbol in our culture.
Most of us in the business community take a certain
egotistical pride in how busy we are. It seems to give
me a certain sense of importance, of self esteem,

knowing my time is in high demand. I routinely postpone luncheon appointments with friends without examining God's priorities for me.

Several years ago, in my final year of the MBA program at Stanford Business School, I had the opportunity to spend a half-hour with Doug Burleigh, now president of Young Life Association. Doug said to me, "If there is one piece of advice that I can leave with you as you approach your entry into the business world, it is this: Go deep into relationships. When you look back on your life later on, you will find that all your business accomplishments are of little value. But the relationships you have taken time to develop will become the most meaningful aspects of your life."

Doug's words have remained with me over the years. As my responsibilities and titles advance, his advice becomes increasingly poignant. As a real estate developer, my income is limited only by the number of properties I develop. The more time I spend nurturing business opportunities, the greater my income and career growth. The challenge God places before me is how to prioritize my time so as not to be consumed by my work.

I set up a list of biblically based priorities in a series of prayerful sessions alone with the Lord, and now apply them to transform my schedule. I am always tempted to divert my attention away from the priorities I set to those "urgent" matters that arise in the business. But God calls me to focus on the "important," not the "urgent." When I succeed at following His call, people are led to Christ, believers grow in Christ, and His kingdom is developed.

CHALLENGE

As Christians, our commitment and love for each other is to set us apart from the world. Love, of necessity, involves community, relationships, and time. Eastern religions tell us that to be "godly" we must separate ourselves from society and become one with the "life force." The Me Generation tells us we need to look out for Number One and take care of our needs first.

Christ calls us to live in community, to love others and place the needs of others above our own. Prayerfully select those relationships that Christ is calling you to focus on, and prioritize your schedule with time to follow His call.

THOUGHT FOR TODAY

If someone examined my schedule, what priorities would be apparent: people or projects, relationships or accomplishments?

by Scott Sellers
Lincoln Property Company
San Diego

SHARPENING MY BROTHER'S AX

As iron sharpens iron,
so one man sharpens another.
Proverbs 27:17

INSIGHT

Behind the obvious and superficial images of people around us are colleagues facing tremendous challenges and problems. We can be a tool God will use in the lives of others.

ILLUSTRATION

A friend of mine was, from all outward indication, a successful financial planner. He owned and ran an organization, had a number of staff members, and was on several boards. Because of his knowledge, he helped a many people move toward their financial objectives. It wasn't until our friendship developed that I became aware he was a fellow believer in Jesus Christ. And I found he was struggling with depression, financial failure, and divorce.

From that point on, whenever I read a passage in the Bible I thought might be uplifting or encouraging, I would call him and share it. When I read something that

I thought might be promising to him, I shared that. I reminded him that our great, marvelous, and wonderful Lord wants to be in control of and at work in his life.

There are people everywhere in the business world who need refreshing information and reminders. The only way they are going to get these reminders is from brothers and sisters in Christ who will take a stand to share Him. This involves a daring step, because once the word gets around you are pegged as one of those religious nuts. But if the attitude and image is maintained consistently, it eventually takes a turn and you become respected and sought out for the stand you take.

CHALLENGE

In the normal course of the day, make it your objective to find opportunities to let business associates know you are thinking about them, are observing their circumstances, and are available to them.

Have one or two passages of Scripture stressing God's promises or God's love ready to share when a situation arises, so you are not caught off guard.

Be a careful listener in your conversations with other people.

Let others know where your strength, and concern come from. Only Jesus can create a burning desire to interact in more than a casual way.

Don't get lured into a dangerous position. Stay in control so as not to be pulled down or conformed to another's circumstances, thereby destroying your testimony.

Rely on the great power that comes from our great God.

Have a positive expectation that something good is going to come out of problems.

THOUGHT FOR TODAY

Winston Churchill said, "A pessimist sees calamity in every opportunity. An optimist sees an opportunity in every calamity." Today I will look for opportunities to sharpen the lives of others.

by Lowell Hartkorn
Johnstown Capital
Redlands, California

LISTEN BEFORE YOU LEAP

He who answers before listening —
that is his folly and his shame.
—Proverbs 18:13

INSIGHT

Sometimes — and usually right when it's needed most
— you come across a verse so clear in its meaning that
the Lord might as well have spoken it audibly. Proverbs
18:13 is like that for me. In my vernacular it means, "If
you answer someone before hearing everything they
have to say, you blew it! Shame on you."

ILLUSTRATION

Though I'd seen this verse often (since Proverbs has 31
chapters, I've found that a great way to jump-start each
day for a month is to read one of its chapters every
morning), it grabbed my attention not long ago when I
was training a key employee new to our business. I like
to keep things moving, and generally don't camp too
long on any given subject. (I was categorized as
"tending toward impulsiveness" when I took the Taylor-
Johnson personality profile test — but what do they
know?) The new employee had lots of questions —
mostly very good ones — but as he asked them, I found
myself anticipating what he would say and interrupting
him to give my answer. I was not only cutting him off,

but also denying him the excellent learning method of framing his questions himself.

As the employee's frustration became increasingly evident, Proverbs 18:13 came to mind. It was obvious Solomon had looked several thousand years into the future, had seen me struggling with this problem, and decided to record a piece of wisdom just for me. I felt I had no other option but to give lis...lis...*listening* (man, that word's hard for me to say) a good old college try. Beginning was the toughest part; for me it included lots of apologies and lots of effort.

I'm still working on this. It's a constant battle. I frequently catch myself moving toward a judgment/disciplinary mode with my children before hearing them out. And of course, I commit this same folly with my wife.

While I've got your attention, could I ask a favor? If you decide to work on this principle yourself and find yourself praying about it, would you say a prayer for the guy Solomon wrote it for? God has my address and I know He'll get it to me — He knows I need it. My wife, kids, and employees thank you in advance (me too).

CHALLENGE

I've been sorry more often for what I've said than for what I didn't say. As business men and women, we're accustomed to thinking ahead, to anticipating what will happen. But when that anticipation shifts from the marketplace to family, friends, and co-workers, and interrupts their communication with us — we're in trouble. It conveys impatience and a lack of respect. In short, it *devalues* others.

Thought for Today

Our Lord Jesus found time to listen to children. People feel valued when I really *listen* (it wasn't as hard to say this time) to what they say, and honor them just as Christ would. Today I will not foolishly give away answers before I know what the questions are.

Or, for you junkyard poets:

> If my tongue goes on the run
> and damage is done;
> I'll bite it.

by Donald C. Jacobson
Questar Publishers, Inc.
Sisters, Oregon

OPEN UP

We have spoken freely to you, Corinthians, and opened wide our hearts to you. We are not withholding our affection from you, but you are withholding yours from us. As a fair exchange — I speak as to my children — open wide your hearts also.

2 Corinthians 6:11-13

INSIGHT

It's not easy to live with open hearts in a world of masks and walls and barriers. God's ways seem inappropriate and unrealistic at times. "Transparency? You don't understand — that's impossible in my work environment. A business person isn't supposed to be vulnerable." We employ various methods to keep others at a distance, to convince them that we are better, more confident, stronger or more self-assured. We all have our finely tuned roles that we've become comfortable hiding behind. But these tendencies are destroying us and our relationships. They also destroy our potential for the Lord.

ILLUSTRATION

The past year has been one of the most difficult of my life. God has challenged me personally to disassemble my walls and destroy the masks I've hidden behind for years. God's greatest work sometimes takes the path of greatest pain. The process has cut deep and at times I wondered who I really am.

The stress created in me by having to be two different people — one a professional business leader with all guards up and masks in place, and another at home and with friends — was exhausting. It was also confusing. Totally different reactions to the same situation would surface in different environments. If I was in my Bible study group I'd react in love. At the office I'd find myself bursting out impatiently, reaffirming my superior position. I found that it took an incredibly humble and contrite spirit to let my colleagues see the gentle person inside and to be as Christ was: a servant.

I found that successful business is based on relationships. There are few positions in the service-oriented business world that are not dependent on people interacting with people. All people ultimately have the same need to be loved, to be respected and to feel significant. When I became the source of these feelings in others, sales increased, customers became more positive, and employees and associates worked harder for me. One or two did not respond immediately, but with perseverance, God's love channeled through a transparent me was overwhelming.

These principles are laced throughout the pages of God's word. Paul, for example, acknowledged his fears, weaknesses, and intense internal struggle with his own sinful heart. He was humble and honest about his strengths and shortcomings, yet continually gave all the credit for his success to the Lord. He survived extreme challenges and circumstances with only God to protect him. This is no different from our professional battles today.

CHALLENGE

Paul's plea for vulnerability applies to you and me. If we are truly committed to making an impact in our world we must let people know us from the "inside out." Satan tells us to protect ourselves by covering up who we really are. He lies! Masks isolate and destroy. If the enemy can keep us distanced from one another as a result of our fears and insecurities, then God's love and blessings remain dormant in a hurting world.

THOUGHT FOR TODAY

God's greatest conduit between Himself and the world is you and me.

by Cindi Kemper
Datatran Corporation
Denver

LIFETIME SERVICE GUARANTEED

Never be lacking in zeal, but keep your
spiritual fervor, serving the Lord.
Romans 12:11

INSIGHT

All major religions offer "something" or nobody would
migrate to them. But what is the key ingredient that sets
Christianity apart? What does it offer that none of the
rest do? SERVICE.

Yes, Jesus serves His followers with a humility and
effectiveness that none of the others can offer.

ILLUSTRATION

I was reading a passage of Scripture on a flight from
Memphis to Dallas one stormy evening. The lady in the
seat next to me was nice enough to ask if I really
believed what I was reading.

"Of course I do," I answered, and without even hesitat-
ing added, "Look at what it says: I can be granted the
power to know the real Christ. Do you see what that
means? It means I can *personally* know Christ and His
power and love, and be filled with His goodness."

Catching my breath, I added, "I notice you have been looking at a pamphlet you are holding. Is it good reading?"

"Oh, yes," she replied, "I know the person who wrote it."

"That does make a difference in how you understand it, doesn't it? That's the reason I love reading the Bible. Because, you see, I know the author."

I have thought about this conversation many times and how it relates to my business. If knowing the author of a book makes a difference in how you read it, then knowing the author of our faith should make a difference in the decisions we make daily. Because I know the Author of my faith, I seek to zealously serve Him by serving people. My endeavor is to be the friendliest, most competent company around and to try to give the best service possible.

The other day I was in Topeka, Kansas, pitching a prospective client on using our services. He asked me a basic question: "What can you do that the other agency can't do?"

"Nothing," I replied, "except give you the service you are entitled to that the other agency isn't doing."

CHALLENGE

Our every business endeavor should be motivated by spiritual fervor. Honor, devotion, and love will become hallmarks of a service-oriented company. As Christians we are basically in the business of serving others because we are servants of the King, Jesus Christ.

THOUGHT FOR TODAY

Car dealers brag about the service after the sale that makes them worthy of your business. How about the service that Jesus provides after you receive Him? It is great to know that I have an Eternal Lifetime Service Guarantee with the God of the Universe.

by George Alban
The George Alban Company
San Jose

CLOSER TO CHRIST

The cords of death entangled me,
   the anguish of the grave came upon me;
   I was overcome by trouble and sorrow.
Then I called on the name of the LORD:
   "O LORD, save me!"
The LORD is gracious and righteous;
   our God is full of compassion.
The LORD protects the simple-hearted;
   when I was in great need, he saved me.
Psalm 116:3-6

INSIGHT

Suffering is sometimes brought on by circumstances over which we have no control, and sometimes by our own willfulness, injudiciousness, foolish risk-taking, mishandling, or misunderstanding. But however pain comes to us, it floods our heart and mind with helplessness and hopelessness. Our Lord would have us learn that especially at such times, we are dealing with a sympathetic Christ.

ILLUSTRATION

Changes in life can feel hurtful, especially those that effect our relationships with people, our health, our comforts, or our lifestyle.

A long-lasting and severe economic depression in our part of the country has left many Christian families with a sickening sense of heartbreaking destitution. The pressure of present-day business and domestic problems wears people down both emotionally and spiritually. Many businessmen are experiencing for the first time in their lives a loss of confidence and a lowered sense of identity and self-worth. Wives feel angry and depressed with real or imagined feelings that their husbands or friends are withdrawing from them.

Having experienced first-hand some of these same feelings, I found that our adversary sometimes over-steps and defeats himself when our overwhelmed hearts cast themselves wholly on God. Never could I express in words all it has meant in my own life — with its spiritual ups and downs, amid quandaries and afflic-tion — to know that I could count on a sympathetic Christ.

This was made comfortingly real to me through many early morning vigils of prayer and study after being awakened with anxious thoughts during long and fearful nights. It was during these precious hours that pain became part of God's plan for me to know His smiting before I could appreciate His smiling. The very things which seemed to break me were really making me. My testings were my benedictions — blessings in disguise. My divinely permitted trials were becoming my triumph as I learned to bear them as a light affliction working for my good.

My Savior became my Comforter, Counselor, Compan-ion. He manifested Himself to me as Sympathizer, Sus-tainer, Satisfier and Sanctifier. None of the good things life has to offer could ever substitute for the riches of Christ discovered in my suffering.

CHALLENGE

Yes, our afflictions work for us and in us. They give scope for the exercise and development of faith. They stabilize and mature us. They lead us to self-examination and purification. They wean us from the world. They call Christian graces into activity. They drive us closer to Christ. They promote separation and holiness. They quicken our desires toward heaven and accumulate for us a corresponding reward as we undergo them faithfully.

THOUGHT FOR TODAY

When we are baffled, stunned, beaten down, weary, dispirited and at the end of ourselves, let us lean on His sympathy to guide our minds and guard our hearts.

by Lawson Ridgeway
Dallas

CHEERLEADERS FOR THE SAINTS

Therefore encourage one another and build each
other up, just as in fact you are doing.
1 Thessalonians 5:11

INSIGHT

Everyone needs encouragement — to find courage to
do and become all that God has in mind for each of us.

ILLUSTRATION

We were losing the most crucial game of the season. I
was seventeen, a cheerleader for my tiny rural Minne-
sota high school. Our guys were discouraged. It looked
like there was no hope (and when you're seventeen,
nothing seems more important than a football game —
remember?) Then we got a good cheer going and
somehow our exhausted team found that extra ounce
of energy they needed to turn the game around.

They needed encouragement. They just needed to be
stretched for success. They needed the support of the
student body to help them pull together to reach for the
goal of winning.

Cheerleading had made a difference in that high school football game, and I think it makes a difference in life.

As leaders we have a challenge to find the right people, place them in the right places so they can perform to their fullest potential, and cheer them on. That can be a tremendous challenge.

If we make our employees feel they are a vital part of the team, they will not only feel great about their jobs, but will convey that excitement to those they deal with throughout the day. Most of us need to be motivated to stretch. It's not something that comes naturally. We need to learn how to motivate others and help them reach their potential.

The number one cause of job stress isn't overwork. It is that we do not feel valued. It is important for our associates to know they are doing their jobs well — and to feel they are fulfilling a higher good than earning a paycheck. Studies show that those who are enthusiastic and are producing results believe their abilities are being challenged and used. Unchallenging jobs result in nonproductivity and a cynical attitude. Peter Drucker maintains most people use only two to five percent of their capabilities. By "cheering people on" we can help them discover and use more of their God-given abilities.

CHALLENGE

There are times when each of us gets discouraged. The best way to pull out of discouragement is to surround yourself with people who are encouragers, who understand the value of affirmation. Get near somebody who believes in you. Discovery always comes in an encouraging environment. Find someone who will help you discover who you are and what you can do.

THOUGHT FOR TODAY

Often the best way to find these encouragers is to become an encourager yourself. Make a conscious effort to encourage someone today.

by Sylvia Nash
Christian Ministries Management Association
Diamond Bar, California

LIVING WISDOM

Enjoy life with the woman whom you love all the days of your fleeting life which He has given to you under the sun; for this is your reward in life, and in your toil in which you have labored under the sun.
Ecclesiastes 9:9, NASB

INSIGHT

Solomon, in a bold venture, deliberately attempted to search out all human wisdom and to understand the source of all folly and madness. He desired to comprehend every deed done under the sun.

Cynical and bitter, he asserted that all man's activities are "vanity," "a striving after wind," and "profitless" (Ecclesiastes 2:11). And yet, even in cynicism he observed two very important exceptions, saying these are your reward in life: the companionship of the woman you love, and the toil in which you labor under the sun.

Solomon added two critical admonitions: "Whatever your hand finds to do, do it with all your might" (Ecclesiastes 9:10), and "Fear God and keep His commandments because God will bring every act into judgment everything which is hidden" (Ecclesiastes 12:14).

In the midst of life's vanities, possibly the wisest man to ever live gives us the guideposts to successful living and true happiness: God, family, and satisfying work.

ILLUSTRATION

Recently a friend had a very important decision to make: to take a one-year sabbatical from his successful business and, with his wife, to devote his labors to a worthy, humanitarian cause they believed in deeply; or to play it safe, keeping his well-staffed office and profitable business flowing smoothly under his direct supervision.

This was not an easy choice. But his business associates rallied behind him and agreed, out of love, to shoulder the extra burdens for that year in order to allow him to pursue this lifelong dream.

A borderline workaholic, my friend and his wife chose to take the sabbatical. I asked him what reasoning finally overcame his resistance. Smiling, with his arm around his wife, he said that a wise friend had reminded him that, "of all the things a man regrets on his death-bed, spending too little time at the office is not one of them."

CHALLENGE

Let us respond with wisdom in a world of vanities: A person may deliberately turn a back to longer working hours, for the benefit of family and those in need. A person may reject a higher-paying job that will give little satisfaction or joy.

THOUGHT FOR TODAY

Under God's authority I will invest the precious
moments of my brief life wisely; first, in loving family
relationships, and second, in work we thoroughly enjoy.

by C. Neal Johnson
First National Bank
Artesia, New Mexico

GOD'S GRACE IN THE HARD TIMES

For the eyes of the LORD range throughout the earth
to strengthen those whose hearts
are fully committed to him.
2 Chronicles 16:9

INSIGHT

It is sometimes easier for us to trust God at the beginning of our career, when we have very little, than it is to trust him after we have reached a measure of success. Yet God is looking for a few good men whose hearts are fully committed to Him. He will allow hard times and difficulties to come our way to see if that commitment is strong. Asa, king of Judah, started out well, yet years of peace and prosperity dulled his commitment, causing him later in life to depend upon his own devices rather than on God.

ILLUSTRATION

For a number of years in my career, I enjoyed the "fast track" which I had often dreamed about. I was committed to my family, our church, and to the Lord. With the exception of some family illnesses, trusting God to provide for us was relatively easy, especially since "the company" was there.

Soon after a promotion and transfer to another office, things began to change. A major business joint-venture began to go sour, and the relationship between my company and the joint-venture partners became very antagonistic. The next six months were the hardest I have ever experienced as personal attacks on my character abounded.

During this time, I found solace in the experiences of David and his cries to the Lord throughout the Psalms. The message became clear to me that God isn't looking for men and women who can help themselves, but rather for those whose hearts are completely His.

After six months of trusting God and trying to set a good example under difficult circumstances, I was fired. My faith was being tested. I was discouraged. Yet only a week later, I found myself with a new business. I dedicated the business to God, but as it grew I began to feel good about myself and my own accomplishments.

When a challenge to my business arose, the old feelings of terror returned. I came back to 2 Chronicles 16:9 and my favorite Psalms, focusing on becoming "fully committed." God was my partner, but I saw that I was the one carrying the stress. I began to see that He didn't want to be just a partner.

I decided that to the best of my ability (some days I do better than others) I am going to give myself and my business to God to do with as He pleases. It is a struggle from time to time, and I am convinced it will always be that way. I know God is there, especially at those times He "phones me up" via some difficulty just to see if I'm still on the line.

CHALLENGE

As Christians in the business world, God calls us to be examples of His grace. Our trust in God, and His working on our behalf, will be made manifest by our response and reactions to difficulties and unfair attacks. God is wanting to strongly support us and to show himself faithful on our behalf. Let us fully commit ourselves and our careers to Him.

THOUGHT FOR TODAY

The eyes of God are upon me. Are my eyes upon Him?

by Bernard Minton
Minton & Associates
San Diego

THE VALUE OF ADVISERS

Plans fail for lack of counsel,
but with many advisers they succeed.
Proverbs 15:22

INSIGHT

The economic forces of the American enterprise system result in owners and executives standing alone at the apex of a production pyramid. I need a group of similarly situated Christian friends to serve as a source of counsel and lateral support to me, even as I likewise serve them.

ILLUSTRATION

A professing Christian who is also a business owner or executive with subordinate employees is sometimes placed in an uncomfortable situation. Consider, for example, the proper response when a church-going secretary mentions she is moving out from her husband and moving in with one of the junior executives (who is leaving his wife), where the situation causes no disruption of the work-flow in the office. Any mention regarding the moral correctness of the situation and you are on the receiving end of a harassment complaint. Ignoring the situation seems an insufficient response in light of the biblical mandate.

In circumstances like this my group of fellow Christian executives is of value to me. They understand the legal strictures and the reality of the workplace. Their counsel is good. All have faced similar problems.

I have access to three such support groups: a weekly Bible study, a monthly breakfast club of Christian executives, and a quarterly Christian book-review group. The discussions in these groups have been rewarding to me, creating a deep understanding of the need for biblical values in our society, and reminding me of the need to purposefully navigate my own Christian walk.

My training and vocation encourage self-reliance. But going solo is not God's plan for my most important job: preparing in this world to live in the next. I need the wisdom and counsel of other Christians so that my plans succeed, and to assure that, if I should fall, there is Someone there to help me up.

CHALLENGE

Today is the day to commence seeking out committed Christian peers to join together in a regularly meeting fellowship group for the purpose of discussing the challenges and stresses I face as a Christian executive.

THOUGHT FOR TODAY

The man who walks in the light of wise counselors will find the pathway to life.

by Paul Dostart
San Diego

EFFECTIVE FAILURES

But one thing I do: Forgetting what is behind
and straining for what is ahead, I press on toward
the goal to win the prize for which God has
called me heavenward in Christ Jesus.
Philippians 3:13

INSIGHT

The foremost deterrent to making a decision is
probably the fear of being incorrect. Effective leadership, however, should allow the freedom to made
mistakes while learning from them. We should not be
paralyzed by past mistakes but should view them as
learning experiences, additions to our database upon
which we can make future decisions as we "press on."

ILLUSTRATION

Following the completion of my postgraduate training,
my first employment was with a small, newly formed
start-up company. After many months of constant
pressure and unreasonable demands, my excitement
with beginning a new adventure was soon replaced by
doubts about the decision. During the next several
years the focus of my attention was so much on the
immediate results of the decision that I completely dis-
regarded the reasons I had made it.

So clouded had my thinking become from all that had transpired that I not only neglected to pursue a sensible strategy to seek out realistic alternatives, but I also nearly made an ill-thought-out choice of walking away from ten years of undergraduate, graduate and post-graduate training to begin a new career in another field.

At the time I failed to recognize that. While the results of my decision were not what I expected, I had gone through a judicious evaluation process and carefully considered the information available. In retrospect, it has become evident that the experience was part of a necessary maturation process that has better equipped and seasoned me to be an effective leader not only in my profession, but also as a husband and father.

Whether or not I made an incorrect decision is not as important as the reasons and process for making the decision.

CHALLENGE

Failures and mistakes will be an inevitable consequence of some decisions because of the limitations of human abilities. But effective leadership should include, in the final evaluation, a careful examination of the process that went into making the decision.

As leaders in our home, work, or church, we should encourage those we are responsible for to develop their decision-making skills by allowing them the appropriate freedom to fail and learn from experience.

THOUGHT FOR TODAY

For those truly seeking to reach their goal, indecision is often the most damaging choice of all available options.

by Bob Wang
Genta, Inc.
San Diego

JOY IN AN UNCHANGING GOD

Consider it pure joy, my brothers,
whenever you face trials of many kinds,
because you know that the testing of your
faith develops perseverance. Perseverance
must finish its work so that you may
be mature and complete,
not lacking anything.
James 1:2-4

INSIGHT

When times are good, it is easy for us to praise God
and be joyful in His providence. However, when times
get tough, He expects no less of a response. God wants
us to rejoice in all trials, not because of the trials themselves, but because of the character and purity they
produce in our lives.

God does not want our intellect, emotions and will to
be controlled by circumstances, but by our knowledge
of who He is, the wisdom He provides to us through His
Word, and our submission to the indwelling Holy Spirit.
When we come to grips with trials, according to His will,
they will no longer distress us, but bring joy instead.

As we endure trials, our endurance will cause us to look
to and trust in Him, to reflect on the eternal benefit of

trials and to enjoy the spiritual growth which He will
bring into our lives.

ILLUSTRATION

Six years ago my wife and I felt led to start a new
business after the company I had been with fell on hard
times. At the time, the job market for my particular
skills and background was depressed, so in seeking the
Lord's guidance we felt a new business was His plan for
us.

The first few years were difficult, and on occasion we
became discouraged. Then a project we had been
working on for more than a year and a half came to
fruition, and the income we received helped us recover
financially. The following year was good.

In this turn of events, we praised God for His faithful-
ness and provision in seeing us through. We thought we
were past this trial and that God would continue to
bless our business.

The next two years, however, were difficult ones. These
matters weighed heavily on me, resulting in deep
searching as to what God would have us do, and more
than a few nights of restless sleep.

Had God changed? No. What was my responsibility? To
walk consistently according to the exhortation and
promises found in James 1:2-4.

I have come to realize that God allowed this trial in my
life for His good purposes. It has resulted in a more per-
severing attitude on my part and a peace of mind
knowing that He is in control. I don't know how long

this particular trial will last, but I know I can continue to come to Him, to seek His wisdom and will. And I know the results in my life will have eternal value. In the meantime I will consider it all joy.

CHALLENGE

We are taught in Scripture to be consistent in our daily walk despite the circumstances around us. We are to be joyful in all trials and to claim God's promises that, in so doing, He will build our endurance with the resultant spiritual growth in our lives bringing praise and glory and honor at the revelation of Jesus Christ.

THOUGHT FOR TODAY

If we are to walk in faith, we need to be consistent despite what we perceive as walls crumbling around us. Am I rejoicing that God is completely in control?

by David Yablonski
American Acquisition Consultants, Inc.
Houston

KEEPING MY FOCUS

Do you not know that in a race all the runners run,
but only one gets the prize? Run in such a way as
to get the prize. Everyone who competes in the
games goes into strict training. They do it to get a
crown that will not last; but we do it to get a crown
that will last forever. Therefore I do not run like a
man running aimlessly; I do not fight like a man
beating the air. No, I beat my body and make it my
slave so that after I have preached to others, I
myself will not be disqualified for the prize.
1 Corinthians 9:24-27

INSIGHT

We need to be self-disciplined leaders who have taken
the time to maintain a clear focus: spiritually, in
marriage and family life, professionally, socially, physically, and financially. We need to run the race to win.

ILLUSTRATION

Many people have remarked to me they wish they could
start their own business. It looks comfortable and glam-
orous, and who hasn't thought at least once of the
advantages of being your own boss? But look beneath
the surface and the real story would be told.

In my case, the price was not small. Trying to keep my marriage, family and business in balance resulted in many 4:00 A.M. work sessions and four years of negative cash-flow, mistakes, sleepless nights, and weekends away from the family.

However, we believed our company and product could make a significant difference and we were willing to pay the price. We had a clear written goal and each quarter we reevaluated our progress, creating new goals, staying focused until we crossed the wire.

If you're like me, watching and reading about success-ful athletes is thrilling; it stirs up the desire to win, to get ahead. I can mentally picture the final laps, crossing the wire, the tremendous human effort which, when consummated, produces Olympic victories. But always remember: Olympic victories require Olympic goals.

CHALLENGE

In the quietness of an early morning, or the solitude of a late evening as you look deep within yourself, consider the race you are running:

- Are you still putting forth the total effort, or have you grown careless?
- Have you maintained a clear focus on the goal, or has this, too, faded?
- Are you running to win or merely to survive?
- Are you denying yourself things which would keep you from doing your best?
- Are you running straight toward the finish line?

THOUGHT FOR TODAY

The greatest single factor in achieving success is having a clear focus. Am I making a disciplined effort to attain my goal with every step I take?

by Robert Smullin
Allergan Medical Optics
Irvine, California

TALE OF TWO MASTERS

"No one can serve two masters.
Either he will hate the one and love the other,
or he will be devoted to the one and despise
the other. You cannot serve both
God and Money."
Matthew 6:24

INSIGHT

The issue here is not money, but deciding who we will
serve. The world would have us make decisions based
upon money and other unstable value systems. Dollars,
yen, marks, francs, pounds, rubles, pesos are all a part
of our lives. How stable are they? What about gold,
silver, oil, stocks and bonds? Newspapers daily report
the continual changes of the world's value system.
These are as unstable as boiling water. Life should not
be lived in constant uncertainty. Decisions and choices
in life and business must be based upon the certainty
of Jesus Christ, who is the same yesterday, today and
forever.

ILLUSTRATION

My business partner and I are constantly tested on this
principle. Once, not wanting to be unequally yoked with
non-believers in business, we walked away from a
project that would have netted us millions of dollars.

Two years later we reviewed the project and realized how the Lord had protected us. Due to greed, soaring interest rates, and a change in the economy our would-be partners had lost everything.

On the second occasion we were not so wise. When a national franchise chain we were involved with had a highly successful year, we went to all lengths to hang onto territorial rights in the financial hotbed of Southern California. In order to maintain the agreement, we pushed, worked and stretched other limits excessively. We had not looked to God and His Word regarding the matter. As it turned out the agreement we sought so hard to hang onto cost us dearly in friends, clients, health and money. We had based our decision on an unstable, changing value system and not on Jesus Christ and His will.

CHALLENGE

Review your schedule for today with the Lord. Ask for His discernment as you go over each event on your calendar. Consider each decision you will be making in the light of Scripture and make clear choices about who you will serve in that context.

THOUGHT FOR TODAY

Don't choose the world's value system. Choose a relationship with Jesus Christ.

by Robert Wattles
PTLA
Walnut Creek, California

GIVING TO GIVE

One man gives freely, yet gains even more;
another withholds unduly, but comes to poverty.
A generous man will prosper;
he who refreshes others
will himself be refreshed.
Proverbs 11:24-25

INSIGHT

From the world's perspective, these verses from
Proverbs cannot be true. Any intelligent person knows
that when you give something away, you have less than
you had before you gave it. Yet the wisest man of all
time, writing under the inspiration of the Holy Spirit,
says the opposite is true: You can give something away
and still have more of it than you did before. Who shall
we believe, economics experts or the God who made
and controls the universe?

ILLUSTRATION

I'm an average guy. When I was twelve years old, I got
my first job in a small grocery store, working after
school. I've worked hard ever since. I married young
and had three children within five and a half years.
After eleven years of managing supermarket meat
departments, I began my own wholesale-retail meat
business at age twenty-nine.

I had been a tither since childhood, but the year I opened my own business, my wife and I sat down with the children and made a family decision to bump our giving up to fifteen percent of our $6,000 yearly earnings. You can guess the result: God began to increase our income immediately — from $6,000 a year to $21,000, then $37,000, $62,000, $85,000, $100,000, and more.

Fifteen years later, we sold our meat business to a larger company, wrapped up our assets in safe, neat investments and went into self-supported Christian ministry for two years. We later heard of the evangelistic work of Christian nationals in foreign countries. Their work is flourishing, and it takes little to maintain national families in full-time ministry (less than a hundred dollars per month in some nations.)

A little fast meat-market-math convinced me I could go back into business, earn money to support these nationals, and multiply myself fifty or a hundred times. I saw that in twenty years, earning and giving fifty thousand dollars per year, we could give a million dollars to God's work.

After making the final decision to do this, I didn't tell anyone for a while because, for an average guy like me, this sounded too good to be true. Well, the short of it is that God did make the million dollar goal, but in His grace and power it took only ten years.

Our current goal is to continue working and giving (at least another million) and to look for a hundred or more other men and women to do the same.

CHALLENGE

God's promises are for average people. God's promise in Proverbs 11 is for all people. It is for you.

THOUGHT FOR TODAY

God's Word is true. You can give...to get...to give...to get...to give. God knows your heart and knows whether He can trust you to end the process on the right word...GIVE.

by Donald Preston
Total Shop SE
Greenville, South Carolina

WITH AUTHORITY

But as for you, continue in what
you have learned and have become
convinced of, because you know those
from whom you learned it, and how from
infancy you have known the holy Scriptures,
which are able to make you wise for
salvation through faith in Christ Jesus.
2 Timothy 3:14-15

INSIGHT

Two people can review identical facts and arrive at
opposite conclusions. Frequently this is not because
the reasoning of one is good and the other is bad.
Rather it is because they start out with different frames
of reference, which cause each to interpret the facts dif-
ferently.

The Apostle Paul instructed his young son in the faith,
Timothy, to continue in the faith from an authoritative
point of reference. Paul goes on to say that all Scripture
is inspired by God and profitable for doctrine, reproof,
correction, and instruction in righteousness so that by
using it as the source of true knowledge we as believers
may be perfect in Christ and prepared to do his good
works.

ILLUSTRATION

I have served as a judge in the State of Texas for over nineteen years: nine years as a trial judge and the last ten as a justice on the Court of Appeals. I must constantly make decisions which affect the lives and fortunes of individuals. The most important issue before a judge is that of authority. What must I follow in reaching the decisions I make? Am I free to do whatever seems right to me as an individual in a particular case, or am I bound by rules which I must apply to a given situation?

A judge takes an oath to support the laws of the state and of the nation. Any judge who places his own feelings above the law, and decides cases on his own whims or personal convictions, is an unjust judge. A judge is bound by the law and not above it. He is bound by the collective wisdom of society as it is codified into legislation, embodied in the basic constitutions of our states and nation, and decided by previous jurists. He is subject to the law. Any person who cannot place himself under this authority should not serve as a judge.

In the spiritual realm there is also an authority. In the history of Christianity there have been four basic types of spiritual authority. They are ecclesiastical authority, tradition, Scripture and human reason. Various individuals have combined these authorities with various emphases.

The apostle Paul was telling Timothy that the written Word of God was to be his authority. All human institutions can and do err. Human reason is fallible and can be used to justify the unacceptable from God's viewpoint. If we do not have a standard by which to check doctrine, we have no authority. If we do not have a revelation of moral absolutes, we each become a law unto ourselves. Bad times fell upon Israel when there was no king and everyone did what was right in his own eyes.

CHALLENGE

Even as a judge must operate under the authority of the law, so also a Christian must operate under the authority of Scripture. We as believers must subject ourselves to His Lordship as revealed through his written Word under the guidance of the Holy Spirit. We should not be controlled by personal desires or ambitions, but by that which glorifies Him and is most effective in bringing other individuals to salvation through the saving blood of the Lord Jesus Christ.

THOUGHT FOR TODAY

When we stand under His authority our lives will be stable, our decisions sound.

by Paul Pressler
Houston

BY WAY OF PAIN

Although he was a son, he learned obedience
from what he suffered.
Hebrews 5:8

INSIGHT

Each of us is called to obedience as children of the
heavenly Father. Yet obedience is often a difficult
lesson to learn. There are times when the only way is
through painful experiences. In pain we are forced
close to Him, until we know that His way is the way we
will go, no matter what the cost.

ILLUSTRATION

After seven years in the Midwest, we had just returned
to San Diego, where we could be with our new grand-
daughter, daughter and son-in-law, as well as live in a
city we loved. I was twelve months into a job as president of a manufacturing company. But it had been my
desire for some time to work for a Christian organization utilizing my education and experiences to help
further the gospel.

After hearing about an opening for such a position that
I was well qualified for, I was excited. This turned to
more realistic thinking, however, when my wife and I
considered the sacrifices of moving again to a distant

city across the country, so I declined to interview for the position.

A few months later it became apparent that my employer was not going to live up to promises he had made when he hired me, and I could not run the business from a Christian perspective as I had hoped to do. I decided to at least try the door to the position with the Christian organization to see if God might be leading me there. The job was offered to me, and after much soul-searching, with my wife in agreement, I gave up my presidency to accept.

We put our home on the market, selling it within three weeks. Later that same week I received a call stating my new position was in jeopardy. The budget for the upcoming year had just been finished, and — based on the results, as well as a change in philosophy — it was doubtful whether they would be bringing me on. Two days later the employer at the manufacturing firm informed me that my replacement had arrived and I should make that day my last. He declined to honor the thirty-day commitment he had given me.

That week was very difficult for us. We had no job and no home. We were confused about the leading of the Lord. We had entered into the decision through much prayer and counsel. Now the desire of our heart appeared to be a dead vision. We persisted in trusting Him even in the darkness. We persisted in prayer and in following His leading as well as we could see it. We were determined to obey Him, to do exactly as He bid us do.

Eventually I found a new job in San Diego and we bought another home we liked as much as the first one. But we wouldn't trade the painful process for all the jobs in the world.

CHALLENGE

Painful experiences help us realize how much God loves us. He cares so much for us, He has a plan for us, and He will take care of us. Am I willing, like Abraham, to go where He leads?

THOUGHT FOR TODAY

God is more interested in conforming me to the image of His Son, Jesus, than He is in my being a successful CFO, CEO, or in whether I'm working full-time in a Christian ministry or the business world.

by Richard Turner
Sail America Foundation
San Diego

PUT OUT YOUR NETS

So they went out and got into the boat,
but that night they caught nothing.
Early in the morning, Jesus stood on
the shore..."Friends, haven't you any fish?"
"No," they answered.
He said, "Throw your net on the right side
of the boat and you will find some."
John 21:4-6

INSIGHT

The call of the Christian is to be faithful. Christ
commands us to cast the net another time. We all tire
of trying. But if we remain committed, if we remain
faithful, the Lord will do His part.

ILLUSTRATION

I opened my datebook to check the evening's appointments. It was staring me right in the face: the one
appointment I would just as soon do without, but I had
scheduled it and I intended to keep it.

Few salespersons really enjoy this type of appointment,
but none can survive without it. My datebook read,
"Tuesday, 6:00 P.M.—9:00 P.M., PROSPECTING."

I have discovered many obstacles and experienced few enhancements from prospecting, especially calling on lukewarm leads. But demands like making a car payment, covering rent, or putting food on the table will make you do the craziest things.

I clutched my notebook filled with numbers from a new telemarketing program and started dialing. Three hours later, and with three-dozen calls under my belt, I had four appointments for the next few days. Funny how so much work seems to lead to so little return.

Sales are comparable to life. You work and work, fighting to make a difference. Progress is hard to come by if you make any at all. The times I feel ready to give up are the times I need to try one more time, to make one more call, to set one more appointment.

One evening after a long day's work I collapsed into our big padded rocking chair and heard myself saying, "I'm done. I've run out of energy, not just for today, but for the entire season. No more. I give up."

Then a still, small voice spoke in my heart. "Throw your net on the right side of the boat."

My wearied soul responded, "Lord, I have toiled all day and for days and nights on end, taking nothing. What good will it do?"

The quiet, yet strong voice continued, "Throw your net on the right side of the boat..."

I wish I could say the phone rang as soon as I was done wrestling with the Lord. The story would end better if I had received an order for a dozen or more products bringing me so much commission that I could barely haul it into my house. Not so. But at that point, it really did not matter. In my conversation with the Lord He reminded me of who is Lord and who is servant.

CHALLENGE

If the master of the sea says stay in the boat and try a few more times, who am I to give up and beach it with an empty net?

THOUGHT FOR TODAY

I was leaving the house for an appointment when I stopped halfway out the door. I looked back at my wife, Robin, and said, "I'm out to make another cast. Say a prayer that I catch something this time."

by Doug Webster
San Diego

GETTING INVOLVED

The LORD said to Joshua, "Stand up!
What are you doing down on your face?...I will not
be with you anymore unless you destroy whatever
among you is devoted to destruction."
Joshua 7:10,12

INSIGHT

The Israelites had been defeated by the city of Ai
because of their own sin. Yet when Joshua, Israel's spiritual leader, cried out in prayer, God informed him it
was no time for prayer, but for action. As crucial as
prayer is, even divine strategy calls for Christians to
sometimes cease prayer and become involved in public
affairs.

ILLUSTRATION

The greatest sin at the crucifixion of Jesus was not
committed by the Roman soldiers, or by the religious
hierarchy, nor even by Pilate or Herod or Judas.
Actually, the greatest sin was committed by the crowd;
they had seen Jesus heal the sick, raise the dead and
cleanse lepers. They knew Jesus was not a criminal.
But despite all this, they passively watched Him die.

Creating an attitude of indifference has been one of
Satan's aims down through the centuries. Our society's

characteristic gesture is a shrug of the shoulders. Its characteristic expression: "Who cares?" The greatest public enemy is not organized crime or communism, but indifference. Social and political programs can never give men salvation, of course, or deliver peace and prosperity on earth. Yet, some Christians use this fact as an easy escape from civic and political responsibility, unwittingly contributing to the deterioration of society.

In Old Testament times, God moved Daniel, Joseph, and Esther into major political positions to protect His people and to influence international affairs. Their role wasn't to force society to adopt their religious convictions. Yet their commitment to God enabled them to serve constituents of every racial, religious and ethnic background far better than leaders void of character and discernment.

Humanists and atheists point to the First Amendment of our Constitution and tell us it means that religion should not interfere with the practice of government. But those of us who acknowledge God rather than man or the state as sovereign in this universe, cannot avoid the conclusion that God's dominion and supremacy must extend over every aspect of life.

We are not true Christians unless we take our Christian principles with us wherever we go. Separation of church and state gives the members of all religions and philosophies, including those who espouse humanist and atheist doctrines, the same opportunity to apply their own values when considering public policy or when participating in the political process. The exclusion of Christian motivation from public affairs only guarantees the political supremacy of non-Christian values. The atheist carries his values with him at all times. Certainly we have no less a responsibility.

CHALLENGE

Christians in America must get involved in fighting godless forces that are making inroads into our local communities. We must involve ourselves in the political process, studying carefully and prayerfully the candidate's records and positions on issues, in supporting measures on the ballot which will truly strengthen the community, the state, and the nation. And, of course, we must pray that God-directed men and women will move into local and national government positions and that Christians already in public office will be given the wisdom, integrity, and courage to pursue their difficult tasks.

THOUGHT FOR TODAY

"All that is necessary for the triumph of evil is that good men do nothing." —Edmund Burke

by James Beam
Beam & Associates
Orange, California

EXCELLENCE
IN THE MARKETPLACE

And whatever you do, whether in word or deed,
do it all in the name of the Lord Jesus, giving
thanks to God the Father through him.
Colossians 3:17

INSIGHT

The first thing the business world identifies with is a
person who is committed to his job, his company, his
associates, and who wants to be successful. I have
found that outstanding business people are exciting to
be around, they are dynamic by nature, and they have a
strong desire to achieve. Couple that person with the
dynamics of knowing God and the strong desire to fulfill
His will and you have a picture of the person God has
called us to be in the marketplace.

ILLUSTRATION

From personal observation (and excuse me for over-
simplifying), I have categorized Christians into three
groups: overachievers, underachievers, and God's
achievers. The overachievers or workaholics look like
their counterparts in the world. They have little time for
family or friends or a relationship with Jesus Christ
because they are working six or seven days a week.

Their spare time is taken up with church board meetings, community service committee meetings, and Christian organization activities. They are so committed to the body of Christ as a functioning organism, that they have forgotten why they are doing these things in the first place. If you were to challenge them, their reply would be something like, "I love what I'm doing," or "I must give my time and talents to the Lord and let Him use my life." The question only they can answer is: "Is my enthusiasm for God's kingdom drowning my love for Him?"

Next come the underachievers, the laid-back Christians. These Christians have no work ethic at all. They demonstrate little desire to move ahead. In fact, they think it is somehow unspiritual even to mention the word *success,* let alone try to achieve it. Legitimate concern about becoming a workaholic turns into failure to put in a hard day's-work. They resist serving on church committees or teaching Sunday School or volunteering time to help in local ministries, with the excuse that they don't want to burn out. If their lives were a true expression of Jesus Christ, Christ might never be seen.

The third group I call God's achievers. They take seriously Paul's admonition to present their bodies as a living sacrifice in acceptable worship of God, conforming not to the world, but being transformed by the renewing of their mind. They want to serve Christ right where they are. They are in the process of developing a lifestyle distinct from that of the world.

God's achievers strive for balance in their lives. They blend their commitment to Christ with a genuine commitment to their business and the people in it. They demonstrate a work ethic second to none. I have come to recognize that the greatest and most effective way I can share my faith is through integrity projected to the people around me. I have learned I need to spend less time talking about my faith and more time demonstrating that I am the kind of person God wants me to be.

CHALLENGE

Many people in the business world would not be open to the gospel of salvation were you to share it with them verbally. But they will watch your life. Your business ethic and personal habits will demonstrate who you are. You have every right to be enthusiastic about who you are, and to bring that enthusiasm into your business. When you have done that, you have earned the recognition and credibility that will cause other people to listen to what you have to say.

THOUGHT FOR TODAY

Young Life, a Christian ministry to high school kids has a motto: "You must earn the right to be heard." This is also the bottom line in the marketplace.

by Jeffrey Comment
Helzberg Diamonds
Kansas City

RENEWING MY MIND

Do not conform any longer to the pattern
of this world, but be transformed by the renewing
of your mind. Then you will be able to test and
approve what God's will is — his good,
pleasing and perfect will.
Romans 12:2

INSIGHT

To the business professional on the cutting edge who's
trying to make a significant difference, the question,
"Am I buying into the world's ways?" is a tough and
vital one. Am I accomplishing my goals God's way? Am
I using biblical principles to the utmost effectiveness?

ILLUSTRATION

The bestselling motivational books talk a lot about the
principal of visualization. They say you must be able to
visualize a task successfully accomplished. Further, you
need to keep that picture in mind until the success is
actually achieved.

I began this practice early in my business career. At first
my visualization was of successfully taking a customer
through a selling presentation and consummating the
order. Most recently my use of daily visualization is
focused upon my communication approach with indi-

viduals, and upon maintaining the utmost integrity regarding my finances.

In any area of struggle, I take seriously God's invitation to allow Him to transform my problem and myself by renewing my mind. Over the past twelve years I have applied this discipline. It works. And I can say from personal experience His ways truly satisfy.

CHALLENGE

Choose an area you need to work on. Write a brief word picture positively stating the task successfully accomplished on a 3 by 5 card. Review this card twice daily. This is critical. Each time you review it, you are picturing yourself successfully accomplishing the task. You are displacing a wrong attitude and set of behaviors with successful habits and a successful mental picture. Over time, when consistently applied, the successful response will replace the unsuccessful one.

THOUGHT FOR TODAY

I will allow Jesus Christ to renew my mind daily.

by Robert Smullin
Allergan Medical Optics
Irvine, California

THE BONDAGE OF SUCCESS

For through the law I died to
the law so that I might live for God.
I have been crucified with Christ and
I no longer live, but Christ lives in me.
The life I live in the body, I live by faith
in the son of God, who loved me
and gave himself for me. I do not
set aside the grace of God, for if
righteousness could be gained
through the law, Christ died
for nothing!
Galatians 2:19-21

INSIGHT

The life we live after our rebirth is lived by Christ in us
and by faith in Him. Many of us who are business
people or professionals have never learned that the
successful Christian life can not be lived by our own
human capabilities, but only by His Spirit deeply
implanted within our own.

We are no different than those gentile slaves of Galatia.
Encouraged by the legalists and judaizers of their day,
they were setting for themselves a code of conduct, a
set of rules, a list of ethics, a set of values that would
make them look as though they lived a good Christian

life. Paul wrote to them to keep them from implementing religious practices in place of the life of the Spirit.

ILLUSTRATION

In my own life, the more successful I became the more I was looked at as an example for others to follow. I was in the limelight, but I felt empty and progressively further from God. Ultimately, I recognized that although my life and success by the world's standards was grand, I was far from His purpose. At that point I cried out to God to align me with His purpose, and I stopped asking Him to bless what were strictly my own goals.

It is a great deception to believe God will bless us if we try to please Him with a goal-oriented drive to be good, do good, try harder, and live out successfully our own established values. And of course, if we fail to live up to the high standards we set for ourselves, we come under self-condemnation. For a time I suffered under this self-condemnation so intensely that I became incapable of sharing my faith.

There was a time when I thought that because of my capabilities, I had to exceed the productivity and goodness of others in order to please God. Now I realize that God wants me to stop relying on my own talents and to instead rely on Christ's life in me.

CHALLENGE

We are not just saved by Him, then expected to lead good lives on our own. We are a new creation in Christ Jesus. We should not be trying to get something we already possess, but remember that we already have all spiritual blessings in Him.

THOUGHT FOR TODAY

Let us not live in bondage to the goals and standards of worldly success, but rather live by the very life of Him within us. The only real success we can ever have is that of total dependence on Him.

by Paul Scheibe
Britton Capital Corp.
Solana Beach, California

IF CHRIST WERE MANAGER

The Spirit of the Lord is on me,
  because he has anointed me
  to preach good news to the poor.
He has sent me to proclaim freedom for the
  prisoners
  and recovery of sight for the blind,
to release the oppressed,
  to proclaim the year of the Lord's favor.
  Luke 4:18-19

INSIGHT

Here is a job description drafted by the Creator of the universe to be fulfilled by the Son of God. The wilderness temptations still fresh on His mind, Jesus entered the synagogue in Nazareth and read this portion of Scripture from Isaiah 61. Every job description must answer three basic questions: "What's my job, who do I report to, and how am I doing?" Have you ever wondered, "How would Christ run this company if He were here?"

ILLUSTRATION

"The Spirit of the Lord is on me" — I have a couple of managers I don't particularly enjoy. I view them as walking umbilical cords waiting to plug into me and

drain my emotional energy. I have to prepare myself
before I meet them. I do two things: Make sure my
attitude is harmonious with His Spirit, and pray specifi-
cally for these managers. If God's Spirit doesn't anoint
me fresh each day, I can expect interpersonal conflict.
Experience has shown this exercise isn't a luxury.
Could you imagine a secular job description that has as
a first priority to check your attitude? Pretty creative!

*"Because he has anointed me to preach good news to
the poor"* — Poverty is not limited to finances. People
can be poor in energy, relationships, ideas, knowledge,
emotions, experience, and spirituality. Many times the
opportunity to share the good news is opened or closed
by the degree of willingness to share other kinds of
good news, showing not only that we care, but care
enough to help. Few people are trying to help others
succeed. Those who are have the respect and ear of
those they are helping.

*"He has sent me to proclaim freedom for the prison-
ers"* — What kinds of things hold people captive?
Whatever they serve: position, power, performance,
materialism, leisure. Employers who are able to create
a visionary attitude in their people set them free to
perform out of their heart, not just out of duty.

"And recovery of sight for the blind" — Have you ever
lost perspective? The symptoms are evident in questions like "How did I get here?" "Where am I going in
this job?" "Is this what I want to do?" "What will I
become?" "I can't see my way out of this." Blindness is
the inability to gather light and to focus. When Jesus
said, "I am the light," He was talking about the eternal
perspective by which we see and measure all of life.

"To release the oppressed" — How are ruts created? By
trudging over the same ground over and over. When the

rut gets too deep, we can't get out and get on with it. We lose hope. When you lose hope, you enter depression. In a rut, we almost always need someone to reach down, pull us up, help us to get on with our lives. Sometimes it's just little things done sincerely and consistently that make a difference.

"To proclaim the year of the Lord's favor" — What year is the year of the Lord's favor? Every year is. So is every day. God never loses control. God is sovereign; He will never allow you to be put on the shelf. In God's eternal economy there are no recessions, depressions, or inflation. None of His deals go sour; they all pay dividends. He relates to us in an unlimited partnership. Every year is a growth year. Every year is favorable.

CHALLENGE

For the next week, read over this job description daily and ask God to internalize it as your own. Seek His anointing through the Holy Spirit as you make your home and workplace a place of freedom and creativity.

THOUGHT FOR TODAY

Have you been through the wilderness? He lured you there in order to speak to you. Is there a shadow over your life? It is the shadow of His wings. The wilderness and the shadows are part of the process He is using to get you ready for the anointing.

by Glenn Plate
A.L. Williams
San Diego

GOD'S RESOURCES — AND YOURS

They all ate and were satisfied,
and the disciples picked up twelve basketfuls
of broken pieces that were left over .
Matthew 14:20

INSIGHT

In this familiar account, the disciples were instructed by Jesus to feed the multitudes who had gathered to hear Him teach. With obvious consternation they replied that they had only five loaves and two fish. Jesus then took the five loaves and two fish, blessed them and gave them to His disciples to distribute to the multitude. When all had eaten and were full, there were twelve baskets of fragments left over.

The issue here — as well as in our life — is not the adequacy of our resources. The issue is God's willingness and delight in taking our obviously inadequate resources to meet the needs of others.

ILLUSTRATION

Well-educated professionals generally believe they have much to offer society. A physician facilitates healing. An architect designs a skyscraper. A lawyer extricates a client from a complex legal situation. Professionals are accustomed to being paid for their knowledge in a specific field. Payment fixes a value to our services. Unfortunately, self-esteem is often tied to such a monetary value. We see our importance graded according to the skills on which others depend. This belief sometimes carries over into our Christian life, making us think our skills and resources are of great value to God.

However, as I reflect on the story of the feeding of the five thousand in Matthew 14, I increasingly realize we have nothing to offer God but obedience itself. I impede God's work most when I fall into the mistaken belief that my personal resources are adequate, that God needs me and that I can do something for Him. In reality, I am most useful to God when I realize my own resources are totally inadequate, that I can do nothing to help God, and that He does not need me. Out of His love and grace He chooses to use me; He chooses to let me participate in His divine work.

It is the sweet paradox of the Christian faith that God works best with broken vessels; those are most filled who realize they are empty; those are richest who understand they are destitute without God. Like the disciples, we may be able to identify a need. The disciples first response was not, however, to ask Jesus to enable them to meet the need. We are to recognize our dependence on Him, and His divine resources to multiply our meager supply.

CHALLENGE

There is a worldly response, taking into account only available physical resources. But God challenges us to visualize what He alone can do.

THOUGHT FOR TODAY

Just as Jesus broke the five loaves and two fishes, He will often allow our resources, whether weak or strong, to be broken. Then He will use them to meet the maelstrom of needs around us.

by William McCurine
Cray, Cray, Ames and Frye
San Diego

BRAIN FILTERS

Finally, brothers,
whatever is true, whatever is noble,
whatever is right, whatever is pure,
whatever is lovely, whatever is admirable —
if anything is excellent or praiseworthy —
think about such things.
Philippians 4:8

INSIGHT

This verse provides a checklist of filters through which my thoughts should be processed. I am exhorted to dwell only on matters that pass certain tests, and if they do not, they are not worthy of my concentration.

ILLUSTRATION

This verse was too encompassing for me to handle all at once. I tackled it piece by piece, taking one phrase each day for a week.

Day One: *"whatever is true..."* Just for today I determine to avoid exaggeration, white lies, misleading statements, innuendo, unverified rumors, or *anything* that might mislead.

Day Two: *"whatever is noble..."* Just for today I determine to think with reverence, honor,

respect, and purity about each person that
passes my way.

Day Three: *"whatever is right..."* Just for today I
determine to think on what is Godly, virtuous,
and decent. I will avoid trite conversation and
foolish talk.

Day Four: *"whatever is pure..."* Just for today I will
seek out holy people, untarnished thoughts,
chaste behavior.

Day Five: *"whatever is lovely..."* Just for today I will
look for inner beauty in the people I meet and
thank God for the loveliness He created everywhere.

Day Six: *"whatever is admirable..."* Just for today I
will think about the people I look up to and
respect. I will meditate on their best qualities.

Day Seven: *"if anything is excellent..."* I will be in
search of excellence all day long. I will avoid the
short cut, the sloppy attitude, the unfinished
task. (That was a tough one for me, and still is.)

Day Eight: *"if anything is praiseworthy..."* The final
thought filter requires that I think about things
that will inspire joy and praise to well up in me.
If it does not, it's not worth spending time on.

After trying this exercise for eight days, I became more
aware of my thoughts, actions, and words during the
hectic interruptions of my life. Random thoughts
suddenly became identifiable. I made them subject to
the riggers of scriptural standards. I became sensitive
to the times my tongue became critical or my mind
wandered out-of-bounds.

CHALLENGE

Try this exercise for the next week. But I warn you: It could be habit forming. And if carried to extremes, you just might become like Jesus.

THOUGHT FOR TODAY

I will make lofty thoughts my highest priority, and fill the treasuries of my heart with their bounty.

by Charles Morgan
Attorney at Law
Miami

THE GREATEST ADVENTURE

What good is it for a man to gain the whole world,
yet forfeit his soul?
Mark 8:36

INSIGHT

Most people do a great deal of planning for their lives
on earth by arranging for their education, career, home,
medical needs, insurance and leisure time. On the
other hand, these same people give hardly a thought to
their eternal destination, failing to assure theirs will be
with God and in His glory instead of in the darkness of
hell from which there will be no escape.Our lifespan on
earth is but a snap of the finger compared with eternity.

ILLUSTRATION

The materialistic comforts of spacious homes, boats
and tennis court, well-paying jobs, delightful vacations
and foreign travel have characterized my lifestyle since
childhood. Despite these enjoyments, however, I did
not experience fulfillment. At times I thought I was
going to have a nervous breakdown.

To find satisfaction and peace in life, I resorted to
alcohol, sleeping pills, tranquilizers and the pleasures

of the world. None of them helped a bit. My life was a dead end.

Eventually, I learned and obeyed the invitation of Jesus to those who are weary and heavy-laden. In desperation, during a health crisis, I turned to God for rest. I decided to become a Christian. I confessed and repented of my sins and asked Jesus Christ to be my Savior and Lord. This is the most important decision that I ever made. The living Savior offered to me the unfathomable love of God, forgiveness, and eternal life.

CHALLENGE

Develop a close and vibrant relationship with Jesus, the living God. Get to know Him by spending time with Him daily: read and obey the Bible, pray fervently and frequently, worship Him in a true Christian church, fellowship with committed believers, and be a witness for Him. Living for Christ is the greatest adventure any person can embark upon.

THOUGHT FOR TODAY

When we receive and follow Jesus Christ as our Savior and Lord, we are able to discern true value in earthly affairs, and we gain an eternal perspective by which to steer our course.

by Allan Mayer
(formerly of Oscar Mayer & Company)
Paradise Valley, Arizona

ME...GENTLE?

As a prisoner for the Lord, then, I urge you
to live a life worthy of the calling you have
received. Be completely humble and gentle...
Ephesians 3:1-2

> ## INSIGHT

Query the average man on the street about leadership,
and you will hear words like strong, determined, tena-
cious, capable, dynamic, forceful, far-sighted. Yet in
both the Old and New Testaments, we are repeatedly
called to gentleness as wise and godly leaders. Gentleness not only makes us more effective leaders, but also
stronger parents, spouses, friends, and members of the
body of Christ.

"But me...gentle?" we ask; "I suppose I could try, as
long as it doesn't mess up my image!"

> ## ILLUSTRATION

Several years ago, in the midst of mid-life career
turmoil, I found myself facing insurmountable odds;
Jericho's walls wouldn't budge. The harder I blew the
more frustrated I became. Bluster just wasn't getting it
for me. Points of personal strength, such as determination, tenacity, and forcefulness, had actually become
my nemesis. In my own family I was perceived as an

undoer rather than a tender care-provider. And that message radiated to the workplace.

I had been seeking wisdom all right, but gentleness? The thought was startling. *Give me a break; a leader's there to win...and lead, right?*

Then I began to reflect on our Lord. Wasn't it gentleness He exemplified when, alone in the garden, He knew others were not holding up their end of the bargain? Wasn't it gentleness when He insisted the little children be brought to Him, or when He unobtrusively turned the water to wine for the wedding host? This "gentleness" was beginning to sound attractive to me.

But what about the mess He made in the temple? That appealed to me more. Then I came to understand that "being," not "doing," was the real issue. My conclusion: Jesus was consistently a wholehearted, determined, *gentle*man.

These verses became the catalyst for a change in me. I was overwhelmingly convicted to become a leader, a husband, a father, who was *gentle*.

It is an ongoing process requiring constant prompting by God, my family and others. But it's all gain as I strive to emulate our Shepherd, Mary's gentle Lamb.

CHALLENGE

What kind of leader or executive spends his time focused on gentleness? This personality trait is tied to some other parameters: courtesy, patience, mercy, flexibility. Are these traits part of your workday experience?

THOUGHT FOR TODAY

In David's great victory psalm he wrote, "Your *gentleness* has made me great" (2 Samuel 22:36 and Psalm 18:35, *The Living Bible*).

Lord, if I am to prosper, let it be in Your gentle spirit.

by Richard W. Oliver Jr.
Poway, California

GOD IS FOR US

And we know that in all things God works for the
good of those who love him, who have been called
according to his purpose.
Romans 8:28

INSIGHT

For those who walk with the Lord, even disastrous circumstances will turn out to be a blessing.

ILLUSTRATION

It was a beautiful June day. All nature seemed to
rejoice in an expression of new life. My wife and I had
taken advantage of a break in a busy schedule to get
away. No sooner had we arrived at our destination than
the phone rang. The voice on the other end of the line
was ominous: "The plant's on fire."

The plant, opened with considerable fanfare only three
weeks earlier, was a high-tech milk-processing facility. I
had brought together a group of supermarket operators
in a joint venture to build a facility to process fluid dairy
and juice products. We had purchased an existing
plant, completely renovated it, and installed high-tech
equipment. The result was a source of pride for me,

I made two phone calls, verifying the extensive damage, and set out on the journey back home. My initial feelings were of shock and disbelief. I had prayed for wisdom throughout the formulative stages of the project. I had prayed for guidance in the selection of joint venturers. The project seemed to carry God's blessings. Had I misunderstood where God was leading?

As these thoughts raced through my mind, my attention was drawn to the beautiful music coming from my radio and I heard the familiar words: "Through it all...I have learned to trust in Jesus, I have learned to trust in God...I have learned to depend upon God's word." This song, together with the encouragement of my wife, who reminded me that no one had been hurt, and that brick, mortar, and equipment are replaceable, brought comfort. From a human perspective, it brought reassurance that I had personally handled the insurance and knew we were covered.

At the scene, my worst fears were confirmed. All that remained of the object of my pride were smoldering ruins. Employees stood about, concerned about their future. My partners and the owner of my company expressed grief. But God reaffirmed in my spirit that all was under control.

I called our insurance carrier to alert them to the loss, and I received another shock. Someone within our organization had, the previous week, erroneously cancelled several million dollars of insurance. It was apparent that my partners might have to sue me and my employer to cover their losses. In addition, I didn't know where we would get the money to rebuild, pending settlement with the people who caused the fire.

But God did. The fire was an accident caused by someone who had gotten careless with a blowtorch, a representative of a financially strong, well-insured company. There were rough roads winding four long years ahead, but time and again I received confirmation that the child of God is never alone. Three years after the fire we opened a magnificent, highly sophisticated, cost-effective facility where profits exceeded projections.

CHALLENGE

The person who cultivates a vital personal relationship with the living Christ, who has fallen in love with God's Son, Jesus, can be assured God is causing even misfortunes to work together for His good. Trust in the Lord; rely on His wisdom in all things.

THOUGHT FOR TODAY

God is more concerned about the development of my Christian character and my Christian witness than with temporal wealth. He wants me to daily become more like Him.

by Charles L. Collings
Raley's Supermarkets and Drug Centers
Sacramento

COMPETITION

It will be like a man going on a journey, who called his servants and entrusted his property to them. To one he gave five talents of money, to another two talents, and to another one talent, each according to his ability...The man who had received the five talents went at once and put his money to work and gained five more. So also, the one with the two talents gained two more. But the man who had received the one talent went off, dug a hole in the ground, and hid his master's money.

After a long time the master of those servants returned...The man who had received the five talents brought the other five. "Master," he said, "you entrusted me with five talents. See, I have gained five more."

His master replied, "Well done, good and faithful servant! You have been faithful with a few things; I will put you in charge of many things. Come and share your master's happiness!"

Then the man who had received the two talents also came. "Master," he said, "you entrusted me with two talents; see, I have gained two more."

His master replied, "Well done, good and faithful servant! You have been faithful with a few things; I will put you in charge of many things. Come and share your master's happiness!"

Then the man who had received the one talent
came. "Master," he said, "I knew that you are a
hard man, harvesting where you have not sown
and gathering where you have not scattered seed.
So I was afraid and went out and hid your talent in
the ground. See, here is what belongs to you."

His master replied, "You wicked, lazy servant! So
you knew that I harvest where I have not sown and
gather where I have not scattered seed? Well then,
you should have put my money on deposit with the
bankers, so that when I returned I would have
received it back with interest.

"Take the talent from him and give it to the one
who has the ten talents. For everyone who has will
be given more, and he will have an abundance.
Whoever does not have, even what he has
will be taken from him."
Matthew 15:15-29

INSIGHT

Each of us was created by God with our own unique
talents and abilities. In the competitive business environment the emphasis is on beating the competition.
There are at least two types of competition. The first is
where the focus is on what others are doing, and what
we must do (sometimes at any cost) to better them.
The second type is in competing only against ourselves,
focusing on the abilities God has given us and in trying
to maximize them for His glory.

ILLUSTRATION

In my position as national sales director for a large financial services marketing organization there is the usual emphasis on growth, not only in additional clients but in diversity of product and customer satisfaction. Part of my job description is to develop motivational techniques. It has been my experience that the strongest motivational force comes from competition.

I am a participant, an encourager, and a developer of the practice of competition. I know individuals who have used it to grow stronger in their personal, business, and spiritual life, developing positive attitudes and multiplying their abilities. But I have also seen competition become a personally destructive force, creating jealousy, suspicion, and devastating "win at any cost" attitudes.

Everyone likes to be a winner, yet by the world's terms only one competitor can win. The lesson of the parable of the talents is that everyone can be a winner. The servant with five talents doubled it and was praised by the master. He was a winner. The servant with two talents doubled it and was praised, though his production was less than half that of the first servant. He was a winner also.

CHALLENGE

In the business environment where peers and management judge us according to how much we produce or how much money we make, there is a big temptation to develop attitudes that are not pleasing to God. It is not the biggest producer God calls successful, but the servant who puts to use the talents God gave him.

THOUGHT FOR TODAY

I will not compare myself with the successes of others. I am my own best competition, investing my talents for the glory of God and the establishment of His kingdom.

by Doug Hartman
A.L. Williams
San Juan Capistrano, California

THE PRICE OF HONOR

Jabez was more honorable than his brothers.
His mother had named him Jabez, saying,
"...because I gave birth to him in pain."
Jabez cried out to the God of Israel,
"Oh that you would bless me and enlarge my
territory! Let your hand be with me, and keep
me from harm so that I will be free from pain."
And God granted his request.
1 Chronicles 4:9-10

INSIGHT

In his recorded prayer, Jabez asks that God would bless
him, grant him more real estate, guide him, and keep
him from harm, releasing him from the curse of his
name, "Painful." At first glance, the prayer of Jabez
seems like a self-centered prayer. But the surprising
thing is that God granted his request.

ILLUSTRATION

How is it, I wondered, that Jabez had so much pull with
God that he could seemingly pray so selfishly and still
receive everything he asked for? The passage does not
even record any reasonable justification for the
requests he made. For example, he didn't tell God that
he wanted a valuable piece of property on a city corner

so he could start a rescue mission in order to win legions of lost souls.

Why is it, I wondered, that when I prayed that God would provide financial success through business investments I had made, He did not answer my prayers? I had even promised Him I would use my financial gains to "help" Him with Christian ministries to facilitate the winning of the lost. Instead my financial world crumbled under me!

I was a "one-hundred-percent" Christian — I could check off the following on my church record each and every week: Sunday School attendance, promptness, tithing, prepared lesson, daily devotions, attendance in worship services. I busied myself with all kinds of Christian ministries and activities, thinking I was doing a tremendous amount of "good works" for God through my own abilities and resources.

At this juncture in my life, God allowed me to go through a "brokenness" experience. I became terribly discouraged, disappointed and frustrated. I experienced so much sorrow and pain that I finally came to the end of myself, and in hopeless desperation, placed my total dependency upon the Lord. In the end, I recognized this position of closeness with the Savior as the fulfillment of my deepest desires.

CHALLENGE

Jabez was a man of honor, but it was an honor born of pain. When Jabez prayed for God's blessings he was in a position to receive them because he had paid the price.

My times are in the hand of God. The higher and more honorable God would build my life, the deeper must go the foundation.

THOUGHT FOR TODAY

Bishop J.C. Ryle said, "All the most eminent saints in every age have been men of sorrows, and often pruned." A.W. Tozer said, "I doubt if God can use anyone greatly, until He has hurt him deeply."

by Morris Takushi
Honolulu

THE LONG HAUL

Not only so, but we also rejoice in our sufferings,
because we know that suffering produces perseverance; perseverance, character; and character,
hope. And hope does not disappoint us, because
God has poured out his love into our hearts by the
Holy Spirit, whom he has given us.
Romans 5:3-5

INSIGHT

Jesus was beaten, spat upon, humiliated, and ultimately crucified, yet none of this diminished His mission or
His goal. His conviction and perseverance were richly
rewarded through His resurrection and everlasting life.
We cannot expect, nor should we expect, a life without
difficulty. We need to understand and accept the fact
that to strengthen and ready us for eternity with Him,
we may have to face and endure extensive trials during
our short duration here on earth. In order to persevere,
we must have the conviction and purpose of Jesus
Christ and never lose sight of the cross.

ILLUSTRATION

The most traumatic trial and misfortune in my business
career was entering a namesake public corporation into
Chapter 11 proceedings. It was not a self-inflicted

event, having been caused by non-paying partners in both domestic and international oil ventures. The results to us, however, were disastrous.

We were advised by counsel to take Chapter 7, liqui- date, abandon all shareholders and, above all, take care of Number One. I could do none of this. Although oil and gas prices continued to fall during our days of reorganization, we, as a family and as Christian employ- ees, weathered the storm. Gratefully, more than ninety percent of our creditors and shareholders approved the Plan of Reorganization and, four years later, we emerged from Chapter 11.

Of course, no one comes out of Chapter 11 strong and girded for more battle. Prices of oil and gas have contin- ued to decline. However, our faith in Jesus Christ and His faith in us sustains our daily endeavors.

CHALLENGE

We are not short-termers! With His strength, you can look forward to tomorrow in order to fulfill a long-term commitment to Him and your fellow man. We are in it for the long haul.

THOUGHT FOR TODAY

Make every crisis an opportunity to reaffirm your com- mitment.

by Richard Bennett
Denver

SHARED VISION

Where there is no vision, the people perish.
Proverbs 29:18, KJV

An understanding of the corporate vision is at the heart of the difference between a high-performing organization and a low-performing one. In a high-performing organization there is "shared tunnel vision." In the low-performer, lack of vision, foggy vision or split vision may put a lid on performance throughout the organization.

ILLUSTRATION

Although I founded our company with a clear idea of how to provide unique information services to users of market-sensitive information, I lacked formal training in how to clarify and communicate a corporate vision. It cost hundreds of thousands of dollars to learn the lesson.

My understanding of the impact of vision came from a business associate at our own staff conference. We went around the room responding to the question: "Why do I work here?" A veteran journalist who joined our team after fifteen years of experience elsewhere said, "I've had many opportunities to execute my skills and get paid for it. But when I interviewed here, I caught a vision of doing something big and important. I had a clear choice between finding a market for my talent and finding an opportunity to buy into a vision where I could grow as a person."

He and others caught the vision of our company in conversation. A few key men helped me shape the vision and attract others to it. The vision clarified itself, was broadened and reshaped over time to be a driving force that impacted many lives. In the early years there was a special electricity in the air — almost an evangelistic zeal in the heart of our business associates.

The shared vision was continually refined from feedback from our customers at management seminars, at "brainstorming" sessions, and from advisory group meetings. Each member of the team was close to the customer in the understanding of priorities. As we have grown, we put our vision into words. It is an overarching statement of philosophy that guides us today to encourage every division, department and team to have a clear view of the big picture.

CHALLENGE

Here are some of the results of shared vision as a driving force:

- You attract quality people who seek more than employment for pay. They tend to stay longer.

- People are self-energized and work until the day's work is done — from their perspective, frequently well after "normal hours."

- There is emphasis on serving the customer instead of carving up in-house territory.

- People seek responsibility well beyond their current level of competence. They grow. The company grows with them.

- "Positive surprises" result from people doing unexpected things.

- Hiring is easy. The word gets around that this company is doing "big things" and providing growth opportunity.

- A sense of excitement and pride drive a positive morale.

- There is positive peer pressure in the workplace for productivity, attitude and customer sense.

- There is a sense that "I am a builder; it is **our** company."

- Lasting friendships, deep respect and trust develop among those who "buy in."

THOUGHT FOR TODAY

Our vision must be renewed regularly. Committed people must be in place to put "feet" on the vision.

by Merrill Oster
Oster Communications, Inc.
Cedar Falls, Iowa

SHAKING OFF GOLD HANDCUFFS

And whatever you do, whether in word or deed,
do it all in the name of the Lord Jesus,
giving thanks to God the Father through him...
Slaves, obey your earthly masters in everything;
and do it, not only when their eye is on you
and to win their favor, but with sincerity of heart
and reverence for the Lord. Whatever you do,
work at it with all your heart, as working for the
Lord, not for men, since you know that you will
receive an inheritance from the Lord as a reward.
It is the Lord Christ you are serving.
Colossians 3:17-24

INSIGHT

The problem facing many Christians in the workplace
today is an improper understanding of why they are
working and for whom they are working. They view their
jobs primarily as a means for earning money, prestige,
acceptance, power, self-esteem, and purpose.

The Bible, however, sums up our ultimate reason for
working in three words: to serve God. Only as we focus
our efforts on Him can we find true vocational satisfaction and fulfillment.

ILLUSTRATION

I met a man who was senior vice president in a company with hundreds of employees. A six-day, 75-hour work week was standard for him. He had no time for his family, hobbies or any other commitments. When I asked why he continued in such a demanding environment, he held his two arms toward me and said, "I don't know how to shake off these gold handcuffs."

Tragic, but honest. He was paid extremely well, had adjusted his lifestyle accordingly, and saw no way of escaping the bondage he had tacitly accepted. His marriage also broke up. Is it any wonder that burnout is so frequent when ambition takes over our lives, and acceptance of the world's values puts us into bondage?

Unfortunately, Christians are not immune to becoming consumed by their own pursuits. In Matthew 25:21, Jesus reminds us that we are only expected to be faithful in a few things. More often than we like to admit, we get caught up in the busyness-bondage-burnout cycle because we are not able to focus on just a few things — the best things.

I believe the Scriptures are clear: We have, through the Holy Spirit, the power to be productive doing the best things. A missionary, prior to World War II, was offered a huge salary to work for a large oil company. He had lived in the country for years and knew the language and culture well, so the oil producer knew he could be a valuable addition and a key to making inroads in that part of the world. Of course, the man would have to give up his missionary responsibilities.

Without hesitation, he turned down the offer, then another and another, each more fantastic than the one before. Finally, the company officials asked what it would take to hire him. His reply was simple, but indisputable: "It's not the money; the problem is that the job is too small." The missionary understood that he was giving his life to a cause far greater and more productive than anything the oil company could ever offer.

CHALLENGE

As people called to serve God, we are all in "full-time Christian service." The material benefits of work may seem enticing, but we must keep God's purposes foremost in our minds. We can serve the Lord just as effectively in a law firm or on a construction site as we can in a church or on the mission field. If we are willing to let Him, God can use our jobs as a "pulpit" — our unique platform for ministry — where we can demonstrate His love and grace through our actions and attitudes, as well as our words.

THOUGHT FOR TODAY

As we prepare for each new workday, we can put ourselves in the proper frame of mind by asking, "What can I do today that will make a difference for eternity?"

by Ted DeMoss
Christian Business Men's Committee
Chattanooga

ABLE & ACCOUNTABLE

And he said, "Who told you that you were naked?
Have you eaten from the tree that I commanded
you not to eat from?" The man said, "The woman
you put here with me — she gave me some fruit
from the tree, and I ate it." Then the LORD God said
to the woman, "What is this you have done?" The
woman said, "The serpent deceived me, and I ate."
Genesis 3:11-13

INSIGHT

The propensity of mankind to shift responsibility has its
origins in the very beginning of history. The result, of
course, is that this propensity is very much a part of our
sin nature. We see it in all people in all aspects of life,
in unlimited forms and manifestations, from "passing
the buck" and blaming others for our troubles, to not
carrying our share of the load, and so on.

However, the person who is redeemed and restored in
Christ is enabled to behave in a responsible and
accountable way, and further, to go the second mile
and to carry the burdens of others.

ILLUSTRATION

During my involvement in a building rehabilitation
project I discovered that a bathroom did not have a

waste clean-out provided. When I confronted the plumber, he said that the carpenter did not frame out a location for it. The carpenter, when confronted, said it wasn't his responsibility to do such framing without the plumber first putting in the clean-out. And so it goes.

Routinely, my two children, when confronted with some mischief, will respond, "Kristin did it," and "No, Lonni did it." As parents we deal with this, firmly joining the responsible party to the misdeed. Our fundamental duty as Christian parents is to teach our children sound values so they are equipped and prepared to deal with the world as they enter it.

Primitive pagan cultures institutionalized the propensity to shift the blame by appeasement of their gods through sacrifice or ritual worship. As long as crop failures, poor hunting or fishing, or other human failings were perceived to be the result of angry gods, virtually no progress was possible. Such cultures became stagnant and impoverished.

Prospering cultures will have a foundation of individual and corporate will to perceive responsibilities as their own and to set about correcting problems by dealing with true causes. Such cultures must be touched by the influence of Christ because only those transformed by the power of God share the spiritual resources necessary to live out a deep personal sense of responsibility — and to live accountably before others and God.

CHALLENGE

As stewards of God's creation, we should seek to advance God's kingdom by conforming our lives to His will, taking responsibility for our own conduct.

THOUGHT FOR TODAY

Am I willing to be accountable for my circumstances and seek God's grace in living responsibly?

by Laurence Shepard
Park Ridge, Illinois

GOD'S LAW FIRST

Do not be a man who strikes hands in pledge
or puts up security for debts;
if you lack the means to pay,
your very bed will be snatched from under you.
Proverbs 22:26,27

INSIGHT

Christians are to avoid guaranteeing or co-signing loans. Loan guarantees force us to come to the rescue of our "friend," the main borrower, just at the time he proves unworthy. Furthermore, lenders would not ask for co-signers if they did not mean to use them. They are not a "technicality."

ILLUSTRATION

Almost ten years ago, I received a large inheritance and hired consultants to help me. All advised that the development of major industrial real estate would greatly help my tax situation, and I became the money-partner in several large real estate deals. I learned that no bank will do a construction loan or a raw land loan unless all the partners, especially the money-partner, sign "jointly and severally." This means that each one, especially the money-partner, is viewed as if he owned one-hundred percent of the project and owed one-hundred percent of the debt.

On a real estate loan default, the bank will foreclose, and if there is a guarantee, they sell the property for what they can, and go after the difference. On a one-million-dollar loan, I would be liable for not half or sixty percent, but one-hundred percent of the deficiency between what they got out of the foreclosure and the total one-million-dollar value of the loan. My idea that the less-moneyed partners should be forced to pay up their share at the same time I paid mine, would be of no use.

I was really more interested in my charitable, political, and intellectual interests than in the details of real estate partnerships. Then a new financial officer concluded that for all the time and money I'd put into them and all the people hired, these real estate projects had not actually made me any more money than if I had left it all in T-bills.

The result of this was that I had to begin to wind down and work toward the time when I could spend most of my time and resources on the things of God: issues related to applying God's word to our culture, alleviating poverty, and issues of stewardship. It was time for me to practice what I believed.

CHALLENGE

We should avoid co-signing for others. In business, this may keep us from entering into partnerships with people of different financial or credit status from ourselves. If I don't have knowledge and personal interest in the details of a particular type of business, I should not be in it, but should stick to those things I am willing to study enough to learn well.

THOUGHT FOR TODAY

Are we willing to follow God's ways when His laws are quite different from those of our business community?

by Howard Ahmanson
Fieldstead and Company
Irvine, California

BRING ON THE OXEN

Where no oxen are, the crib is clean,
but much increase is by the strength of the ox.
Proverbs 14:4, KJV

INSIGHT

Those who refuse to disturb the status quo will avoid
the little problems that go hand-in-hand with progress.
But if we are willing to take them on, we will reap an
abundant harvest. God is not proposing that we should
take uncalculated gambles or spend money when the
stakes are too high. But God does want us to realize
there is a natural disturbance along with productivity,
and we should not be put off by potential complica-
tions.

ILLUSTRATION

"There might be riots, fights, demonstrations, even
killings!" "The cost would be ridiculous — fifteen
million dollars!" "And what for? Traffic will be tied up
and local residents inconvenienced." "Remember years
ago, the Chicago Democratic Convention? It did the city
more harm than good!"

Remarks like these flew among leaders of the power
structures in Georgia when the city of Atlanta was considering to bid on hosting the 1988 Democratic and

Republican national conventions. What had started as an exciting possibility quickly turned into a series of rebuttals and negative rationalizations.

As president of the Atlanta Convention and Visitors Bureau, I was in favor of bidding on the conventions. My mind was searching for ways to turn around the conversation. Finally, I thought of the Bible verse hanging on the wall in my office: "Where no oxen are, the crib is clean." I quoted the verse to the group of leaders, and for a brief moment I felt like that E. F. Hutton television commercial where everybody falls silent and freezes — people who are eating stop chewing; people walking stop in midair. I thought, *What have I done?*

At last, one of the most respected community business leaders laughed and said, "That's right! This could be a multi-million dollar promotion for the city and certainly there will be problems, but compared to the potential results, it's worth it!" The meeting turned around, and the leaders began to pursue a positive note, putting together a team effort.

Atlanta was chosen to host the 1988 Democratic National Convention. During the week of the convention, the wave of reporters from around the world promoted Atlanta in a dynamic way. To be sure, there was some negative coverage, but ninety-nine percent was positive. In addition, we estimate a billion dollars worth of publicity for the fifteen million dollar investment.

I have found the sign in my office to be a tremendous topic of conversation as I deal with many committees and groups who do not want to do sales and marketing programs if there are any problems associated with the project.

CHALLENGE

Beyond our personal belief in Jesus Christ for the forgiveness of sin and eternal life, we should make Him
our daily reference point by applying His Word in a prac-
tical way on a daily basis.

THOUGHT FOR TODAY

"No manure, no milk...there is a price to pay for productivity" (Ryrie Study Bible footnote to Proverbs 14:4).

by Ted Sprague
Atlanta Convention & Visitors Bureau
Atlanta

GOD'S ARMORY: OUR DEFENSE

Finally, be strong in the Lord and in his mighty power. Put on the full armor of God so that you can take your stand against the devil's schemes. For our struggle is not against flesh and blood, but against the rulers, against the authorities, against the powers of this dark world and against the spiritual forces of evil in the heavenly realms.
Ephesians 6:10-12

INSIGHT

It is not easy to maintain Christlike standards in the fast-paced world of business. We are up against powerful external forces that test our faith on a daily basis. To rely on our own power is useless. But we are not left without help. The whole armory of God is available to us, and with this defense we can stand and thus succeed.

ILLUSTRATION

At the beginning of my walk with Christ, my wife and I announced to skeptical in-laws my decision to enter the world of business as a professional automobile salesman. Mot a typical salesman, mind you, clad in white shoes and plaid sport coat, and presenting a well rehearsed pitch of half-truths. But an honest sales-person who could build a career through professional-ism backed by integrity.

Shortly thereafter I was introduced to the real world by a senior salesman that claimed Christ every third Sunday. He told me, "Doug, to be a good salesman you have to have a little larceny in your soul." I almost quit that day. Even though that statement still occasionally haunts me, I renewed my determination to be different.

Things were not as easy as I imagined they would be. My line of business can lead to conveniently stretched truths for easy sales. Another struggle was dealing with fellow salesmen who were stealing each other's cus-tomers, including mine. I try to deal with these issues as a Christian and to be a witness for Jesus Christ to my co-workers. It has never been easy. I will admit I have failed miserably many times, especially when I have relied on my own strength and not been actively pursuing God.

CHALLENGE

I have found four ingredients to be necessary for me to work effectively as a Christian in business. Check these against the patterns of your life:

- *Prayer.* This is the most important one. Unless I'm in close communication with God, things just don't work out. I need to be talking to God all day long and involve Him in my business and personal life.

- *Accountability to another Christian who knows my business life and personal life.* Several years ago I got involved with a Christian man whom I felt could give Moses a run for his money (at least he might be able to part the water in his bath tub). We developed a Christ-centered friendship. He started praying for my witness at work and for my prosperity. I not only found myself compulsively witnessing, but also being consistently more successful in sales. I didn't even flinch when he told me he would quit praying for me unless I cut him in for ten percent of the action! (I think he was kidding.)

- *Regular involvement with church.* This includes, for me, a weekly Bible study where the relationships developed around God's Word give me balance that flows into my business life.

- *The Word of God.* Recently I have been writing on a 3-by-5 card some Scriptures that apply to struggles I face at work. I carry these with me until I have overcome.

THOUGHT FOR TODAY

Do I focus on this world and just glance at God, or do I focus on God and just glance at the world? Do I modify my Christian principles to fit my business or do I modify my business to fit my Christian principles?

by Doug Gabbert
Gresham Toyota
Gresham, Oregon

BIG ENOUGH?

Trust in the LORD with all your heart
and lean not on your own understanding;
in all your ways acknowledge him
and he will make your paths straight.
Proverbs 3:5-6

INSIGHT

It's easy to absorb ourselves in becoming successful by
the materialistic terms of our culture. We sometimes
forget that success and the accomplishment of our
goals may result in no eternal significance at all. It's
possible to be a resounding success in the world but to
accomplish nothing for God's kingdom.

ILLUSTRATION

As a tax attorney specializing in estate planning, I
spend most of my days meeting with people to discuss
how their "stuff" will be disposed of when they die. I
have had the opportunity over the past several years to
observe their efforts and priorities during their life-
times, to attend their funerals, and then to observe the
disposition of their estates after their deaths.

As I've observed all this, some truths become
inescapable. You can begin to tell at the funeral what a
man's life has amounted to. There are some whose

passing goes barely noticed — men who are alive today and dead tomorrow — and there is hardly a ripple on the sea of human emotion. But others leave an indelible mark on the lives of their fellow men.

As I have seen these differences between those who leave a significant positive impact on the lives of the survivors and those who don't, I've noticed that many multi-talented people work hard on the details of life, but never see the "big picture."

To use an illustration from my own life, at the time of my father's recent death I inherited a trust established by my grandfather, including several stocks. In the best fashion of the 80s, I became an astute equities investor. I tendered, bought, sold, and reveled in the intellectual exercise of the stock market. I applauded myself as a good steward. After about six months of this fascination, I was sitting one night reading the stock quotes in the paper and my wife mused, "This is a new side of you, always reading the stock prices. I liked it better when you came home and talked to me."

I then did what I had failed to do earlier. I sat back and took in the big picture. I envisioned in my own mind what it would be like if I accomplished what I was working so hard at. If I was successful in my investments, then I would die with a large estate. Even if I was able to have the best tax-wise plan, the most I could hope to accomplish would be to leave my children and grandchildren financially secure.

Having observed innumerable financially secure individuals whose lives had no significant impact on others, I knew this would be a hollow victory. If I left only wealthy children who had no love for Christ or for others I would have to consider my life a failure.

I had failed to do what I invariably urged my clients to do: "Make certain you see the big picture before you pursue a goal." With the help of a close friend, I determined to delegate the responsibility for making the investment decisions to a Christian financial advisor, and to spend more time investing in the lives of my wife and four children. I'm not opposed to creating an estate, and I have to say I want financial security, but those are grossly inadequate life goals. At my funeral I want the survivors to say, "He really had a heart for Christ...put his family first...always seemed to have time for you...Why he even prayed with me in his office."

CHALLENGE

Stop right now. Step back and take a good look at your "big picture." Envision the accomplishment of what you are working so hard on. Will actually accomplishing the goals you've adopted have an impact of any eternal significance? Step beyond death's door and listen in at your own funeral. What are people saying? If you are dissatisfied with what they are saying, begin now to make whatever mid-course corrections are necessary. Pray unceasingly for God's guidance to shift your goals to accomplish a life's work of eternal significance.

THOUGHT FOR TODAY

Make certain you have God's big picture before you spend a lifetime in unworthy investments.

by Al Todd
Todd & Johnson
Columbia, South Carolina

ALWAYS SOWING

Cast your bread upon the waters, for after many
days you will find it again...Sow your seed in the
morning, and at evening let not your hands be idle,
for you do not know which will succeed, whether
this or that, or whether both will do equally well.
Ecclesiastes 11:1,6

INSIGHT

We should be ready at all times to sow seeds leading to
eternal life. Even during business hours, our labor can
never be separated from our walk with the Lord. We are
all farmers in the kingdom of God. If we offer the Bread
of Life to people we meet, we never know...their lives
may be part of a successful harvest.

ILLUSTRATION

A friend of mine — a fellow Gideon — had always
attended church and regularly went to Confession. His
real temple, however, was the baseball park, football
field, and basketball court. He never missed a game.
He was a fine citizen and member of the local Rotary
Association.

One day, as he and a guest pastor were leaving a Rotary
meeting, the pastor asked him, "Are you saved?"

My friend was angry and irritated at the question. He was so mad at that pastor he could bite nails. But he never forgot it. Eventually, he came to a fruitful and joyful relationship with Jesus Christ.

One day I was in the home of a client and quoted a Bible verse in connection with our conversation. My client stared at me. "Do you read the Bible?" she marveled.

"Why sure, I read it every day," I replied. "Do you have a Bible?"

She got up and reached to a high shelf, taking down a huge, dust-covered book. "This is my Bible," she said. "But I didn't think it was possible to understand it, so I've never read it."

I opened her Bible up to John 3:16 and read the verse for her. "Can you understand that?" I asked.

"Why, yes," she admitted. I wound up the conversation, finished my business, and was on my way.

Several weeks later I visited her briefly to get a form signed. There were several people sitting around her dining room table so, after getting her signature, I hurried out the door. As I was pulling away from the curb in my car, she ran out into the yard with that big book under her arm. "Wait, Mr. Smith, " she yelled. "Will you show me again where to find that verse we read last time you were here? I want to tell my relatives about it." I showed her and was on my way.

Recently, I retired and moved from the city where I'd done business over thirty years. The day before I disconnected my office phone, this same woman called (I'd had no contact with her for twenty-some years) to thank me for opening her dusty old Bible and, for the first time, exposing her to the simplicity of the Word of God. She told me of the resulting salvation of herself and her children.

CHALLENGE

God doesn't require us to be theologians or Bible expositors. He only asks that we share our faith boldly and consistently. Keep it simple. But sow it morning and evening.

THOUGHT FOR TODAY

People are simply thirsty. If you have discovered the fountain of living water, don't keep it a secret. Pass it around.

by Marvin M. Smith
Fidelity Union Life Insurance Co.
Sisters, Oregon

SCRIPTURE INDEX

THE PROVERBS
IN BUSINESS

On the following pages are Bible study exercises
from the Book of Proverbs. The study topics
represent **key issues in the lives of every
business man and woman.**

In your own time of Bible reading and reflection,
take one topic per day, look up the verses, and
complete the simple exercises (these are designed
in the same format as the chapters you've been
reading in *THE BIBLE IN BUSINESS*).

The Proverbs provide a wealth of wisdom with
direct application in the business arena. Use these
study exercises to help you tap into their riches.

CONFLICTS

Look up and reflect on Proverbs 17:1,
17:14, 17:19, 19:18-19, 20:3, 22:10,
26:17, and 26:21.

INSIGHT

(Key statements and principles in these verses)

_____

_____

_____

_____

_____

_____

_____

ILLUSTRATION

*(How I see the principle at work in the lives of people in the Bible,
in my own life, and/or in the lives of other people)*

_____

_____

_____

_____

_____

_____

_____

_____
_____
_____
_____
_____
_____

CHALLENGE

(What to do or change — in my own life or business)

_____
_____
_____
_____
_____
_____

THOUGHT FOR TODAY

(The best "handle" to help me remember the principle)

_____
_____
_____
_____
_____
_____

Today's date: _____

FAIRNESS

Look up and reflect on Proverbs 17:15,
17:26, 18:5, and 23:10-11.

INSIGHT

(Key statements and principles in these verses)

_____

_____

_____

_____

_____

_____

ILLUSTRATION

*(How I see the principle at work in the lives of people in the Bible,
in my own life, and/or in the lives of other people)*

_____

_____

_____

_____

_____

_____

_____

_____
_____
_____
_____
_____
_____
_____
_____

CHALLENGE

(What to do or change — in my own life or business)

_____
_____
_____
_____
_____
_____

THOUGHT FOR TODAY

(The best "handle" to help me remember the principle)

_____
_____
_____
_____
_____
_____

Today's date: _____

FOR YOUR OWN STUDY AND REFLECTION

PERSONAL INTEGRITY
PART I

Look up and reflect on Proverbs 11:1,
11:3, 12:17, 14:2, 14:5, 14:11,
14:25, and 15:8.

> ## INSIGHT

(Key statements and principles in these verses)

_____
_____
_____
_____
_____
_____

> ## ILLUSTRATION

*(How I see the principle at work in the lives of people in the Bible,
in my own life, and/or in the lives of other people)*

_____
_____
_____
_____
_____
_____

_____
_____
_____
_____
_____
_____
_____
_____

CHALLENGE

(What to do or change — in my own life or business)

_____
_____
_____
_____
_____
_____
_____

THOUGHT FOR TODAY

(The best "handle" to help me remember the principle)

_____
_____
_____
_____
_____
_____

Today's date: _____

PERSONAL INTEGRITY
PART II

Look up and reflect on Proverbs 16:11,
16:17, 19:5, 20:17, 24:28-29,
28:10, and 29:10.

INSIGHT

(Key statements and principles in these verses)

_____

_____

_____

_____

_____

_____

_____

ILLUSTRATION

*(How I see the principle at work in the lives of people in the Bible,
in my own life, and/or in the lives of other people)*

_____

_____

_____

_____

_____

_____

_____

CHALLENGE

(What to do or change — in my own life or business)

THOUGHT FOR TODAY

(The best "handle" to help me remember the principle)

Today's date: _____

WEALTH

Look up and reflect on Proverbs 10:15, 10:22,
13:8, 13:11, 15:27, 18:11, 21:17, 22:7, 23:4-5,
27:23-24, 28:6, 28:8, 28:11, and 28:22.

INSIGHT

(Key statements and principles in these verses)

_____

_____

_____

_____

_____

_____

_____

ILLUSTRATION

*(How I see the principle at work in the lives of people in the Bible,
in my own life, and/or in the lives of other people)*

_____

_____

_____

_____

_____

_____

_____

_____

_____

_____

_____

_____

_____

_____

CHALLENGE

(What to do or change — in my own life or business)

_____

_____

_____

_____

_____

_____

_____

THOUGHT FOR TODAY

(The best "handle" to help me remember the principle)

_____

_____

_____

_____

_____

_____

Today's date: _____

MY WAY OF SPEAKING

Look up and reflect on Proverbs 10:19,
12:23, 13:3, 15:28, 17:27-28, 18:13,
21:23, and 29:20.

INSIGHT

(Key statements and principles in these verses)

_____

_____

_____

_____

_____

_____

_____

ILLUSTRATION

*(How I see the principle at work in the lives of people in the Bible,
in my own life, and/or in the lives of other people)*

_____

_____

_____

_____

_____

_____

_____

_____
_____
_____
_____
_____
_____
_____

CHALLENGE

(What to do or change — in my own life or business)

_____
_____
_____
_____
_____
_____
_____

THOUGHT FOR TODAY

(The best "handle" to help me remember the principle)

_____
_____
_____
_____
_____
_____
_____

Today's date: _____

DILIGENCE

Look up and reflect on Proverbs 10:4-5, 10:26,
12:11, 13:4, 16:26, 18:9, 19:15, 19:24, 20:4,
20:13, 21:5, 21:25-26, 22:13, 24:27,
24:33-34, 26:14, and 26:16

INSIGHT

(Key statements and principles in these verses)

_____

_____

_____

_____

_____

_____

_____

ILLUSTRATION

*(How I see the principle at work in the lives of people in the Bible,
in my own life, and/or in the lives of other people)*

_____

_____

_____

_____

_____

_____

_____

_____

_____

_____

_____

_____

_____

CHALLENGE

(What to do or change — in my own life or business)

_____

_____

_____

_____

_____

_____

THOUGHT FOR TODAY

(The best "handle" to help me remember the principle)

_____

_____

_____

_____

_____

_____

Today's date: _____

GETTING COUNSEL

Look up and reflect on Proverbs 11:14,
12:15, 13:10, 15:22, 19:20,
20:18, and 24:5-6.

INSIGHT

(Key statements and principles in these verses)

_____

_____

_____

_____

_____

_____

_____

ILLUSTRATION

*(How I see the principle at work in the lives of people in the Bible,
in my own life, and/or in the lives of other people)*

_____

_____

_____

_____

_____

_____

_____

_____

_____

_____

_____

_____

_____

_____

CHALLENGE

(What to do or change — in my own life or business)

_____

_____

_____

_____

_____

_____

_____

THOUGHT FOR TODAY

(The best "handle" to help me remember the principle)

_____

_____

_____

_____

_____

_____

_____

Today's date: _____

ANGER

Look up and reflect on Proverbs 14:17,
14:29, 15:18, 16:32, 19:19,
22:24-25, and 29:22.

INSIGHT

(Key statements and principles in these verses)

_____

_____

_____

_____

_____

_____

_____

ILLUSTRATION

*(How I see the principle at work in the lives of people in the Bible,
in my own life, and/or in the lives of other people)*

_____

_____

_____

_____

_____

_____

_____

_____
_____
_____
_____
_____
_____

CHALLENGE

(What to do or change — in my own life or business)

_____
_____
_____
_____
_____
_____

THOUGHT FOR TODAY

(The best "handle" to help me remember the principle)

_____
_____
_____
_____
_____
_____

Today's date: _____

GOD'S GUIDANCE & PROTECTION

Look up and reflect on Proverbs 16:4,
16:9, 19:21, 20:24, 21:30-31,
and 22:12.

> INSIGHT

(Key statements and principles in these verses)

_____

_____

_____

_____

_____

_____

_____

> ILLUSTRATION

*(How I see the principle at work in the lives of people in the Bible,
in my own life, and/or in the lives of other people)*

_____

_____

_____

_____

_____

_____

_____

_____

_____
_____
_____
_____
_____
_____
_____

CHALLENGE

(What to do or change — in my own life or business)

_____
_____
_____
_____
_____
_____
_____

THOUGHT FOR TODAY

(The best "handle" to help me remember the principle)

_____
_____
_____
_____
_____
_____

Today's date: _____

GOD'S GUIDANCE & PROTECTION

Look up and reflect on Proverbs 16:4,
16:9, 19:21, 20:24, 21:30-31,
and 22:12.

INSIGHT

(Key statements and principles in these verses)

_____

_____

_____

_____

_____

_____

ILLUSTRATION

*(How I see the principle at work in the lives of people in the Bible,
in my own life, and/or in the lives of other people)*

_____

_____

_____

_____

_____

_____

_____

BIBLICAL PRINCIPLES FROM THE PROVERBS

_____

_____

_____

_____

_____

_____

_____

CHALLENGE

(What to do or change — in my own life or business)

_____

_____

_____

_____

_____

_____

THOUGHT FOR TODAY

(The best "handle" to help me remember the principle)

_____

_____

_____

_____

_____

_____

Today's date: _____

DR. RON JENSON, the compiler of *The Bible in Business*, is the president of High Ground Associates, a worldwide association of business and professional leaders.

High Ground seeks to expand the strategic spiritual impact of these leaders by providing access to the best resources and services available, including books, tapes, videos, consultants, advisers, and organizations. High Ground thus serves leaders as a "one-stop shop" for resources with biblical values.

High Ground also offers seminars on "Life Values," "Biblical Success," and "Ethical Leadership."

Dr. Jenson travels widely to speak about values and leadership at conventions and other business and professional events.

For more information, call or write:

High Ground Associates
11590 West Bernardo Court, Suite 230
San Diego, California 92127

(619) 487-2766